D0079202

WITHDRAWN

UNDERSTANDING
Mary Lee Settle

Understanding Contemporary American Literature

Matthew J. Bruccoli, *Editor*

UNDERSTANDING
Mary Lee
SETTLE

By GEORGE GARRETT

UNIVERSITY OF SOUTH CAROLINA PRESS

Published in Columbia, South Carolina, by the
University of South Carolina Press

Manufactured in the United States of America

Library of Congress Cataloging-in-Publication Data

Garrett, George P., 1929–
  Understanding Mary Lee Settle.

  (Understanding contemporary American literature)
  Bibliography: p.
  Includes index.
  1. Settle, Mary Lee—Criticism and interpretation.
I. Title.   II. Series.
PS3569.E84Z67   1988   813'.54   87-25469
ISBN 0-87249-540-X
ISBN 0-87249-541-8 (pbk.)

For Nano
Who has not, until now, had a book all her own.
With love and gratitude. Always.

CONTENTS

EDITOR'S PREFACE

Understanding Contemporary American Literature has been planned as a series of guides or companions for students as well as good nonacademic readers. The editor and publisher perceive a need for these volumes because much of the influential contemporary literature makes special demands. Uninitiated readers encounter difficulty in approaching works that depart from the traditional forms and techniques of prose and poetry. Literature relies on conventions, but the conventions keep evolving; new writers form their own conventions—which in time may become familiar. Put simply, *UCAL* provides instruction in how to read certain contemporary writers—identifying and explicating their material, themes, use of language, point of view, structures, symbolism, and responses to experience.

The word *understanding* in the series title was deliberately chosen. Many willing readers lack an adequate understanding of how contemporary literature works; that is, what the author is attempting to express and the means by which it is conveyed. Although the criticism and analysis in the series have been aimed at a level of general accessibility, these introductory volumes are meant to be applied in conjunction with the works they cover. Thus they do not provide a substitute for the works and authors they introduce, but rather prepare the reader for more profitable literary experiences.

M. J. B.

UNDERSTANDING
Mary Lee Settle

CHAPTER ONE

Understanding
Mary Lee Settle

Career

After World War II, in which she had served first of all as an aircraft woman second class in the Women's Auxiliary of the Royal Air Force, then later in the (American) Office of War Information in London, Mary Lee Settle returned to America and was hired for the editorial staff of *Harper's Bazaar*. One day in late summer of 1945 she came back to the office after a leisurely luncheon to find on her desk a layout of photographs of the Brontë country, together with a copy of the Modern Library Edition of *Wuthering Heights*, which she was supposed to use to put together appropriate captions for the pictures. A moment of literary epiphany. "I realized that Emily Brontë had written it and was dead by the time she was twenty-eight," Settle has written. "I had just turned twenty-seven. So I saw my two ways. Either I would still be sitting there, a well-paid fashion and arts editor at forty, still writing about other people's accomplishments, or I would plunge into the precarious world of writing myself."[1] That was the moment of her conversion, her commitment to the art and craft of writing. Beginning in 1946, when she went back to England, she lived and supported herself, hand to mouth ("I was entering dedicated poverty as into a door"[2]), not by any regular or full-time job, but mainly by free-lance journalism of various kinds, including some bits and pieces as "Mrs. Charles Palmer," an etiquette expert for *Woman's Day*. Hard years of apprentice writing, six full-length plays and many short stories, without any of it except the journalism being published. From one of her plays, *Deeds* (now lost she says), she created a novel—*The Kiss of Kin*. But no publisher in Britain or America was interested enough to accept it. "Then I wrote *The Love Eaters* as a result of a bet with James Broughton," she has written. "I said tragedy required recognition by the audience; he said it was inherent. So I said that if the Phaedra were in a modern setting she would be treated as comic, pathetic, menopausal, but not tragically."[3] Elsewhere she has pointed out, and not without irony, that "no critic has ever recognized the plot of the Phaedra, which has something to do with proving the old argument."[4] The novel was accepted by Heinemann in London on 30 October 1953. It was published by Heinemann in Britain and Harper in America in 1954, receiving good notices. The following year both publishers bought out *The Kiss of Kin*. Mary Lee Settle was now a novelist.

UNDERSTANDING MARY LEE SETTLE

Settle was born in Charleston, West Virginia, on 29 July 1918. Though her roots are deep in both Virginia and West Virginia, much of her early childhood was spent in Kentucky, where her father owned a coal mine, and a little later in Florida, where, a trained civil engineer, he went to find work during the Florida boom. In the depth of the Depression the family came back to West Virginia to live in her grandmother's house in Cedar Grove. "I went to school in Montgomery on the school bus," she writes, "and on winter mornings I saw the miners going to work in the dark with their carbide headlamps lit and at night I saw them coming home in the dark."[5] Later they moved back to Charleston, and there Settle took elocution lessons from an elderly gentleman named Maurice Drew, who proved to be the first of a number of deeply influential teachers. She writes: "He opened up a world to me that somehow met the inner world that I had thought was completely isolated."[6] Her second important teacher in those days was Sara Spencer, an actress of real talent, crippled by polio, who encouraged her toward acting: "She made me speak over and over, long past suppertime, until she had forced me into losing myself in a part, and when I had done it at last, she knew it, and for the first time I knew it, as one knows whether in writing, or acting, or sports, or music, or painting, when one has found true pitch."[7] At eighteen Settle was sent off to Sweet Briar College in Virginia, an experience which is the center of what she calls "the only autobiographical novel I have ever written, *The Clam Shell*."[8] There she came to literature through another outstanding teacher—Joseph Dexter Bennett. "He handed me poetry, and then walked away and let me explore it for myself."[9] Following her second year at Sweet Briar she found work in the summer at the Barter Theater in Abingdon, Virginia; and she was one of a number of young American actresses tested and seriously considered for the role of Scarlett in the movie version of *Gone with the Wind*. After that, she writes, "I did not go back to Sweet Briar. Went the rounds to agents to get a job as an actress in New York that winter of 38–39 and earned my living modeling. First for Powers and then for Harry Conover."[10] In the summer of 1939 she married an Englishman, Rodney Weathersbee; and when war broke out that fall, she and her husband went to Canada, where he joined the Canadian army and where her son and only child, Christopher, was born. She and her husband never lived together again and were divorced in 1946. By the end of 1941, with America now in the war, she left her child with family in West Virginia and tried to enlist. The American women's services would not take her because of her less than perfect eyesight, but the British were not so demanding. She crossed by convoy to Britain, where she joined the WAAF, an experience she has recounted in *All the Brave Promises: Memoirs of Aircraft Woman 2nd Class 2146391* (1966).

Since the publication of *The Love Eaters* Settle has worked steadily as a novelist, living both in America and abroad (England, Italy, Greece, and Turkey), working at miscellaneous jobs when she has had to, including some journalism and teaching at Bard College, Iowa, and the University of Virginia. She has thus far produced ten more novels, two books of nonfiction, and two juveniles. In 1965 a play of hers, *Juana La Loca*, was performed Off-Broadway at the American Place Theater.

In terms of recognition and reward hers has been a career of ups and downs. She likes to point out that she has been "discovered" (then, of course, forgotten) a number of times. The low point, in her view, came in 1976 when, while she was a visiting lecturer at the Iowa Writers' Workshop, she was urgently rewriting her novel *Blood Tie*, for which she could not find a publisher. "I was without a publisher after 10 books and over 20 years of publishing," she told Myra MacPherson in a *Washington Post* interview.[11] In early 1978 she won the National Book Award for *Blood Tie*. "What the award meant to me," she has written, "was a reunion with the literary world, advances seven times what they had been before, and acceptance of what I was doing."[12] It also meant, in the short run, some disappointment and trouble. There was an unpleasant journalistic tempest-in-a-teapot as various professional book reviewers, who had not in fact yet read *Blood Tie*, protested the award. The fuss died down quickly as soon as they had read the book. It was a wound, but she had long since trained herself to take the bitter with the sweet. In a piece about her life in England during the 1950s, just as her professional career was beginning, Settle shows how she has come to terms with the double-edged dangers of critical reputation:

> No writer I know who has achieved a reputation after years of work has escaped having it thrown back in his or her face. I am reminded of the young, poor poets trashing T. S. Eliot in London pubs in the early Fifties, or young would-be novelists decrying the reputation of Graham Greene, Henry Green, Somerset Maugham, Angus Wilson, too, or any other famous writer who had succeeded after long years in that most unforgivable of activities—earning money and critical acceptance.[13]

"A good review stops me working for about three days," she has said elsewhere, "and a bad review stops me working about four days. I've long since learned to just get on with it."[14] Something else, an early experience and understanding, helped to sustain her. In the fall of 1953, shortly after the acceptance of *The Love Eaters*, she was present at a luncheon with Somerset Maugham, Alan Searle, and Angus Wilson, who was meeting Maugham for the first time. She had met him once before, doing a journalistic interview piece on assignment, and it had been a pleasant experience. This time, fly-on-the-wall, she observed Maugham at his worst, arrogant with his guests and savage in his gossip and appraisals of the leading writers of the time. "My idols and mentors fell, one after another," she writes. "It was like that all through lunch, every remark weighed and weighed again, all the signs secret among the English, the Literati, and the Accepted were brought

UNDERSTANDING MARY LEE SETTLE

out, tested, some found wanting, some passed, as the cheese."[15] After the luncheon she went for a long walk in Hyde Park and tried to come to terms, within herself, with what she had seen: an honored public man whose face was "etched with years of pain and bitterness." Adding that she realized that "I could help being etched as he was by acceptance or denial. I saw that it was not fame itself, but the seeking of fame that could destroy." And she arrived at serious resolutions: "I vowed to find my energy from within and not from reputation and to avoid the 'literary' life. I resolved to be grateful for understanding and praise and honors if they came, but never to hang on to them, and after what books I would write, how many of them I had no idea of, to forget publishing as soon as I could and get back to work."[16]

More serious, in the year following her National Book Award for *Blood Tie*, was a battle with cancer which she won. "I was in the middle of writing a book," she says. "I had to get back to work."[17]

Since then there has been no slowing down, no diminishment of her productivity. Three major novels—most recently, at this writing, *Celebration* (1986)—have appeared. And Scribner's Signature Editions has begun the process of bringing out all of her earlier fiction in trade paperback editions. Already *The Love Eaters*, *Kiss of Kin*, and *Blood Tie* have appeared in the series, and the others will follow. In a significantly generous gesture to aid other writers, Settle created, then sponsored and raised funds for, the Pen/Faulkner Award for Fiction, an annual national prize judged exclusively by fiction writ-

UNDERSTANDING MARY LEE SETTLE

West Virginia and with the fictional town of Canona (modeled after Charleston). *O Beulah Land* begins shortly after the Fort Duquesne massacre of 1755, flashes back to London in 1754, and then moves chronologically forward through the time of the French and Indian Wars and up to the summer of 1774, just as the struggle which would soon enough become the American Revolution was about to begin. *Know Nothing* concerns the years 1837–1861, that period which led directly into the tragic bloodbath of the Civil War. *The Scapegoat* is built around the beginnings of a coal strike in 1912 but also includes significant sequences set later, notably one in France in 1915 during the Battle of the Somme. And even though it is set mainly in 1978 and in 1980 in West Virginia, *The Killing Ground*, as the conclusion of the quintet, has a very wide range of time and allusion, including not only all the time covered by the other novels, but also glimpses into much earlier history as well. Thus, essentially, the sequence of novels runs in narrative time from the seventeenth century to the present. All of them are linked together, first of all by an intricate network of families, a circuitry of generational connections, close and distant kinships and blood ties. The principal family names are Lacy/Lacey, MacKarkle/McKarkle, and Catlett, but there are many other relationships among minor characters. Some of these connections are fully known and understood by characters in the midst of events; others are available only to the reader with full access to the entire chronicle. Critic Rosemary M. Canfield has noted some of the things that serve to join the novels of the quintet together: "The four later books in the series are all set in the same area, and all five of the novels shared the same family and Christian names, in varying conjunctions; the same character traits, appearing in men and in women; the same conflicts; and the same themes, embodied in the changing face of history."[19]

The Beulah quintet will be treated in more detail in the following chapter of this study. At this point, however, it needs to be noted that, in and of itself, the quintet is an extraordinary achievement. No other serious American novelist of Settle's generation—that generation which came to literary prominence in the years following World War II—has chosen to attempt anything so large and ambitious. Certainly no other American novelist of her generation set out to create a work of fiction so large and ambitious. Some writers of the earlier generation—Faulkner, for instance, with his Snopes trilogy and the more loosely interrelated Yoknapatawpha novels and stories—clearly planned works of at least similar breadth and scope. But Settle's remarkable accomplishment stands alone in its time.

In honoring and appreciating her artistic success one should always bear in mind that, in a practical sense and in many significant details, the literary life of her generation in America has proved to be substantially if not radically different from the first half of the century. Without belaboring this somewhat peripheral point, it needs to be understood that, just as the society of the United States was in many ways different and possessed

UNDERSTANDING MARY LEE SETTLE

by different values (both good and bad) from a contemporary point of view, before World War II and in the years following after, so the publishing business has changed significantly with the times during the same period. The ways and means of writers have changed to meet the altered realities of the relationship of writer to publisher. By and large, and with some significant exceptions, publishers are no longer interested in building long-term careers, in the slow and steady (and traditional) accumulation first of works, then of reputation, which literary history teaches us that serious writers require. Again with some notable exceptions, most serious American writers have had to move from publisher to publisher until, if they were lucky, they have finally managed to achieve some kind of "breakthrough." During the almost thirty years the making of the Beulah quintet required, Settle was published by a number of different hardcover publishers in America—Harper, Viking, Seymour Lawrence/Delacorte, Putnam, Houghton Mifflin, Random House, and, finally Farrar, Strauss and Giroux. This not atypical history covers a multitude of disappointments and dashed hopes. Speaking not out of any self-pity, but for all other serious and dedicated writers, she has written strongly about some of the negative aspects of contemporary publishing: "I think that there is one thing beyond all others that is unpleasant to the point of evil about producing a book. Not the hard work. Not the lack of reward—but the actual process of publishing itself. It ought to be a decent time. Instead it is obscene. A whole industry depends on us and treats us like shit."[20] No question that the complexities of the contemporary publishing scene made the completion of such a major undertaking as the quintet a difficult and risky process at all levels. That she persisted, managed to do the work and to see it published, is astonishing, a genuine cause for wonder and admiration. "You lose plenty of faith in *yourself*, but not in the book," she has said. "In the quintet, I had a subject so powerful it wouldn't let me go."[21]

During the same period she was also writing other books, the other novels which, while separate from the quintet, are equally serious and are in fact related to the quintet in a number of ways. Place holds her work together. Critic Nancy Carol Joyner has noted some of the connections of place (and family) in other novels. "*The Kiss of Kin* (1955) takes place in a house close to the Canona River, and two other novels, *The Love Eaters* (1954) and *The Clam Shell* (1971), are set in the town of Canona and include many of the same characters that appear in *The Killing Ground*, such as the Dodds, the Potters, the Slingsbys, and Charlie Bland."[22] In fact everything but *Prisons* and *Celebration* is at least referential to Settle's part of the upper South, genteel Virginia and hardscrabble West Virginia. Even *Blood Tie*, which is firmly placed and deeply set in modern Turkey, offers some vividly evoked scenes in Virginia, partly as background and partly for contrast. In all of her work, and increasingly so as she has grown and developed as a novelist, place is urgently important, a force in and of itself. Where things take place matter a great deal. *Celebration*, though chiefly set in the London of 1969, also contains major narrative units which take place in Turkey, East Africa, and Hong Kong. Place is one of the things *Celebration* is about; the diverse places, so significantly different, become unified, becoming one wholeness, a sum composed of many distinct places, our single planet, when the central characters from all over the world gather together at a festive party to see the moon landing on television: "The room was full of the bright light of Houston. They heard the scratchy voice from the moon say, 'The Eagle has landed.' Somebody had repeated it. Teresa heard '. . . on the Sea of Tranquillity,' and she was afloat in the Sea of Tranquillity in the middle of a room gone mad."[23]

If intense concentration on place and the sometimes most complex and subtle relationships of very different places, each to the other, are powerful elements in Settle's art, then so is time, a very precise sense of time and its impact within the texture of the past, history, and of any given present moment. Her characters act in that given time and react to it; acting truly in that they are never given a view over the horizon of the present into the future. One may know what is coming, what is in store for them; but they see what they see and know what they know. And what is honestly important to them may be trivial to the reader. Thus the regicide, the execution of Charles I, which changed England and the nature of the monarchy forever from the long view, causes only a slight ripple and inspires no prophetic present about its past to recover the essential and specific uncertainty of the past in its own bright moment of happening. In this case they are remembering the coronation of Elizabeth II, and Noel tries to explain something of what being a homosexual meant then and there in England:

> However many were cheering and carrying on that day about the Queen, there was many another poor queen of England quaking in his boots. 1953 was a bad year for queens, whatever you might think. *Agents provocateurs* in drag in the Underground, raids on clubs like this, friends up in the Central Criminal Court of the Old Bailey for obscene libel because they wrote about the existence of love between men without the necessary derisive terms—bugger, faggot, bum boy, poof, queer, fairy, pansy—yes, dearie, I was and am, God knows, and He does, all of those (167).

A third element giving her work in all its variety a coherence and wholeness, one that has often been remarked by reviewers and critics and indeed other writers, is her use of characters, her ways and means of characterization. Each of the books, in whatever time and whatever setting, is unusual for the number and variety of dimensional characters. She seems to be able to present wholly credible characters of every race, creed, color, age, national origin, and sexual preference. She appears to be in no way limited by social class or background. Her Turks, Africans, Chinese, English-women and Scotsmen—all are fully imagined and manage to be credible representatives of whatever group they may belong to while somehow transcending collective stereotype to become memorable individuals. This great skill (one is tempted to call it magic) of hers would be unusual at any time in the history of the novel, but it is even more so now when the most trendy postmodern fiction has turned away from characterization altogether, and even more traditional writers have by and large accepted the widespread, and often selfserving, sociopolitical notion that they are not free to imagine and write outside of the most reductive limits of their own superficial experience. Thus old people write about old people. Blacks write about blacks and whites about whites. Artists are expected, often *required*, to accept and embrace the very specific and limited parameters of their autobiographies. Fiction, like confessional poetry, becomes interesting and engaging depending, more or less, on the facts of the life, the author's life, behind it.

Of course, some of the more imaginative writers have given themselves a little more elbowroom by inventing, out of whole cloth, interesting fictional lives for themselves. But Settle writes as if she never heard of this problem. It is also clear that, never trendy or fashionable, she writes as if she had no interest whatsoever in the intricate games of postmodern metafiction. Which is not entirely correct. In conversation she has often praised the work of her friend, the postmodern metafictionist par excellence, Robert Coover. And she has used, albeit for very different purposes, a complex fusion of autobiographical fact and fiction in *The Killing*

UNDERSTANDING MARY LEE SETTLE

Ground, which is a characteristic of some metafiction. But in theory and by practice she is deeply concerned with the creation of solid characters, and with the use of language, a translucent language, for that purpose as much as any other, to liberate her characters to be themselves.[24] Her success in characterization is great. If there are any flaws and failures, they usually involve minor characters who have no more than fleeting opportunities to escape the shackles of their type or, sometimes, characters with whom the author is so fundamentally at odds that she cannot develop them much beyond the cartoon-strip level. Frank Proctor, the clumsy CIA agent who appears in both *Blood Tie* and *Celebration*, is an example of this. But part of the reason that some minor and lesser characters seem less dimensional and more stereotypical than others is a tribute to the success with which she has created the memorable individuals at the center of her fictions. The lesser figures, who cast no shadows, tend sometimes to stand out oddly and alone.

These things—the power of accurately evoked place, the precision of exactly recalled and re-created time, whether contemporary or historical, and the development and exploitation of dimensional characters—are acts of the imagination, wholly engaged, concentrated upon fictional events; and they come together to give Settle's work a singular coherence. Taken with other qualities they form what may be called the signature of her art. From the work itself, as well as from a variety of more or less secondary sources, including her own articles and book reviews, lectures and interviews, one can discern two general, separate, and yet related and simultaneous guidelines to the appreciation of her art: first, her theoretical aesthetic, that is, her foundation of critical ideals and models, her aesthetic assumptions; and, second, her practice of the craft of fiction, a practice which for most serious contemporary writers, though it may be based on certain rules, is rooted in deep intuition, not fully conscious, certainly not *self-conscious* in its initial (first draft) stages, but arrives at that kind of awareness gradually in the rigorous interrogative stages of revision. Perhaps surprisingly for an artist who has emphasized the ineffability and mystery of the beginning of the process, Settle has nonetheless described and defined her own experience in some detail. For her the beginning is an image, a brief flashing vision which not so much captures as commands her attention. She has said that all of the Beulah quintet began for her with the image of one man hitting another man in the drunk tank. She saw and felt that moment and wanted to know why. Five books and twenty-eight years later, with *The Killing Ground* she came to her answer.

In her introduction to the Franklin Library's First Edition Society edition of *Celebration*, she speaks of this initial vision in some detail, beginning with the proposition that "I am not ready until a concept is transmuted into a sensuous vision so clear that it is like a remembered reality." Before vision and behind it was the raw material of experience, a basic concept waiting to take form: "I have had cancer, and I wanted to explore

UNDERSTANDING MARY LEE SETTLE

survival, and getting on with life. I knew that some-where within me, my wartime experiences and this experience met and fused and informed each other—not in the actions themselves but in the reactions to them." Continuing, in the same brief piece, she offers a simple and straightforward account of the arrival of the myste-rious angels of vision: "The first vision came in the middle of dinner with Ann Beattie in the fall of 1982. She says that I told her I had to leave because I was going to write a novel. I don't remember. I do remember borrow-ing paper from her and sitting in my car and writing down glimpses of a woman alone making a list. That was all. The next image was of a small group of people gathered in London and celebrating the death of Charles I. Between these two visions was *Celebration*."[25]

In a memorandum about the teaching of writing, composed at Bard College sometime during the middle 1960s, Settle presents that most mysterious and difficult to articulate moment—"The beginning, the function of inception itself, the turning of silence into words"—about as sensibly as anyone has been able to do. Building her perceptions on the foundation of analo-gous comments by her special literary heroes, Proust and Conrad and Eliot, and the image of the descent within the self, she writes:

The difference between the descent that brings back some-thing totally other than has been before, and the philosophic descent is that this one is unaccompanied and brings back new images and new names rather than new concepts or new views of the already existent. It is not harder, but it is rawer, more unguided and riskier, necessarily disordered and frequently daemonic.

The inarticulate, the daemonic, the lonely place. It sounds by these directions mysterious and subtle, dangerous and taboo. Indeed, it is unsafe. It deals, if it is any good always with the unknown, only and often fearsome to those who have not lived and worked at that edge. It deals with newly constructed visions and the reporting of them. It deals with what has not yet been made.[26]

Settle may be almost alone among American writers in strongly believing that the right teacher in the appropriate context can help students at this stage of the creative process. "It cannot be taught," she writes, "but the circumstances, the preparation in which it can make the leap into words can be taught; the patience, the quiet, the listening, can be simulated if you like in the studio so that the unknown becomes, not less unknown, but less fearsome, and less weighted with expectation." The next stage of the process she describes here, is the editing, "a process of looking behind the first tentative words at the vision itself and asking of what is on the paper, did I tell the truth? Is it this way? Does this word or this phrase tell what I saw there? Good editing at this stage does not work by critical negation, but at its best by an almost Socratic method of questioning." As she conceives it, the editing process can be worked out alone, but may be collegial; it is a stage where writers, and good readers, can and have helped one another. The third, last step is critical, in

UNDERSTANDING MARY LEE SETTLE

which "the critic has the function to take it from his hands." She adds that the critical function is profoundly important.

In a more recent piece Settle has described her "influences" as Conrad and Proust ("I call them my teachers, too").[27] Here she also cites and honors her friend Roger Shattuck as the prototype of the exemplary critic. Her affinity with Shattuck, a distinguished scholar and critic of French literature and culture, points toward another special aspect of Settle's fiction. The greatest part of her work has been specifically concerned with American history and the American experience. *Prisons* points forward, giving the background and the basis of conflict for the characters in the other four volumes of the Beulah quintet. *Blood Tie* and *Celebration* present major American characters in the context of a larger world and thus help to define that experience by comparison and contrast. But Settle sees herself as being outside the limits of "the high wall of modern American writing." "I am a highly sophisticated stylist," she writes, "for good or ill, with my roots in Europe after seventeen years of living and working there and being exposed to the subtlety and structure of English and French writing." It is this different angle of vision—an inner conflict or tension, if you will—classic American raw material being processed by someone who is very close to her material in every way, by experience and inheritance, and yet at the same time refined by her discovery of and extended exposure to other ways and means of transmuting vision into art; it is this quality which gives to her work an added coherence, the unity of a single and singular point of view. She has said, as noted, that only one novel, *The Clam Shell*, is "autobiographical." And elsewhere she has insisted that only two characters in all her work are, in deepest fact, autobiographical—separately and equally Johnny Church in *Prisons* and Lily Lacey in *The Scapegoat*.[28] But in a larger, if looser, sense all of her work, including journalism and minor pieces, is so personal (after all, it begins in every case with the intimately personal experience of an image or vision) as to be autobiographical. Her fiction, more than that of many of her peers, is an attempt to render, not to disguise or camouflage, an authentic version of her inner life.

One other aesthetic singularity deserves consideration. Settle was thirty-five years old when her first novel was published. Not old, by any means, for a first novelist; but she had been working for years in journalism and editing, writing poems and stories and plays. She arrived more experienced than most first novelists, and *The Love Eaters* and *The Kiss of Kin* are exceptionally professional and well executed. They are controlled, well made and well wrought, so finished in form that they give few hints of any future directions the artist might take. These two books, advanced in mastery of craft, have not become dated much, if at all; yet she changed. Already, even as her first books were being published, she was deep into *O Beulah Land*. And when that appeared in 1956, she says that she lost the literary admirers of her "acerbic" modern manner in the first

UNDERSTANDING MARY LEE SETTLE

books while gaining others, different reviewers and a different audience.[29] The movement and growth of her art has been steadily toward more freedom, more daring structures, more "experimental" adventures in the art of fiction. Which, at the least, is the opposite of the direction of many other serious writers who start in innocent freedom and gradually learn control.

In the complex marriage of themes and values her work demonstrates an unusual sense of unity. From the first until now she asks many of the same questions. Freedom, the full exercise of it and the abuse or loss of it, has been one of her chief concerns. Rosemary Canfield sees the conflict of freedom against four kinds of enslavement—by authority, by received and accepted social hierarchy, by social and economic systems, and by personal obsessions—to be crucial in the Beulah quintet and in her other work.[30] Certainly conflict, most often revolution against forms of enslavement, is one of her primary subjects. Her identification with Johnny Church and Lily Lacey, each in a different way a radical and revolutionary, is significant. There is also the paradox, which she shares with the young man and the young woman, of being a revolutionary from a "good" family; being a person of excellent, indeed refined tastes, choosing a way of life where taste is scarcely relevant. Accurately described as "always a vociferous liberal,"[31] she has shown a passionate consistency of viewpoint, arguing, as she does in her autobiographical essay, that "all those who have stood against the misuse of power, whether in Prague, in Chicago, in Chile, in

Warsaw, or Nixon's United States, have fought the same battle. I saw that the fight is not between the right and the left, but between democracy and authoritarian government, no matter what it calls itself or where it is found."[32] It is the latter part, the second sentence, which so modifies her thinking as to prevent it from being a purely reflexive liberalism. She means it when she announces her opposition to all forms of antidemocratic authoritarianism. Thus she surprised a good many people when she spoke at the American Writers Congress in 1981; arguing that "complacency is the constant enemy of the democratic process," she devoted her talk to criticizing covert forms of censorship in the publishing industry, defined as censorship by distribution, censorship by management, and finally the self-censorship of the writer, in part the result of "a dark shadow of fear within our own minds" and in part coming out of "literary snobbery," which only serves to stifle or inhibit "the bright vision that is the reward of the courageous worker at the top edge of talent and energy."[33] Finally, among her most strongly held and consistent values has been her religion. She describes herself as "a closet Christian . . . now out of the closet."[34] This last, the sense of "coming out," refers to her creation of the highly positive and admirable character, Pius Deng, an almost-seven-foot black African Jesuit priest who figures as the true hero of *Celebration*. Looking back to the beginning, one can see that her work has always set the values of courage, compassion, and integrity against hypocrisy, indifference, and above all lack of charity. And it is clear now that something spiritual, an ancient and traditional form of Christianity, has shaped her understanding of human folly even as it has informed her vision of human possibility.

Notes

[1] Settle, "Mary Lee Settle," *Contemporary Authors Autobiography Series*, ed. Dedria Bryfonski (Detroit: Gale Research, 1984) 1:313.

[2] Settle 314.

[3] George Garrett, "Mary Lee Settle," *Dictionary of Literary Biography: American Novelists since World War II*, ed. James E. Kibler, Jr. (Detroit: Gale Research/Bruccoli Clark, 1980) 283–84.

[4] Settle, 315.

[5] Quoted Garrett 282.

[6] Settle 309.

[7] Settle 310.

[8] Settle 311.

[9] Settle 311.

[10] Garrett 283.

[11] Myra MacPherson, "Mary Lee Settle, Forthrightly," *The Washington Post*, 15, Jan. 1987, C9.

[12] Settle 321.

[13] Settle, "Maugham," unpublished typescript 17.

[14] Tim Kerr, "Author: Novelist Settle Maintains Success without catering to 'Fashions,'" *The Daily Progress* (Charlottesville) 30, Oct. 1986, D6.

[15] Settle, "Maugham" 11.

[16] Settle, "Maugham" 14.

[17] Kerr D6.

[18] MacPherson C9.

[19] Rosemary M. Canfield, "The Beulah Quintet," *Masterplots II*:

UNDERSTANDING MARY LEE SETTLE

American Fiction Series, ed. Frank N. Magill (Englewood Cliffs, NJ: Salem Press, 1986) 153.

[20] Garrett 282.

[21] MacPherson C9.

[22] Nancy Carol Joyner, "Mary Lee Settle's Connections: Class and Clothes in the Beulah Quintet," *Women Writers of the Contemporary South*, ed. Peggy Whitman Prenshaw (Jackson: University Press of Mississippi, 1984) 167.

[23] Mary Lee Settle, *Celebration* (New York: Farrar, Straus, 1986) 239. Page numbers in parentheses refer to this edition.

[24] This is most fully discussed in the American Audio Prose Library tape cassette *Mary Lee Settle: Interview* (June 1982).

[25] Settle, "A Special Message for the First Edition from Mary Lee Settle," *Celebration* (Franklin Center, PA: Franklin Library, 1986). See also Settle, "Life is really a dance,"*US News and World Report*, 22, Dec. 1986; 64.

[26] Settle, "An Inquiry into the Teaching of Writing as an Art," unpublished typescript, C-4.

[27] Settle, "Mary Lee Settle" 322.

[28] *Mary Lee Settle: Interview.*

[29] *Mary Lee Settle: Interview.*

[30] Canfield 157–58.

[31] MacPherson C9.

[32] Settle, "Mary Lee Settle" 319.

[33] Culture Industry (tape cassette), American Writers Congress 9–12 Oct. 1981, New York City.

[34] MacPherson C8.

CHAPTER TWO

The Beulah Quintet

For the general understanding and appreciation of the Beulah quintet there are a number of good, authoritative sources. From her various interviews, from the lengthy autobiographical essay she wrote for *Contemporary Authors Autobiography Series*, and from some of her articles, produced for various purposes, there is a considerable and strikingly consistent body of information about the origins of this series of novels, both individually and collectively, about the process of creating the novels—where and when and how she worked on them, including some of the ways she went about doing the kinds of research necessary—and what her general aims were. With the final volume, *The Killing Ground*, she has given, within the limits of that story and by means of some fairly daring fictional devices, at once a recapitulation of the whole series and a reflexive summary and commentary on it. The single volumes must, of course, stand as novels on their own, in and of themselves, as well as functioning as coherent parts of

UNDERSTANDING MARY LEE SETTLE

the larger design, the whole quintet. Nevertheless, the readily available information about the author and her goals and intentions is enormously helpful, enhancing the experience of the entire series.

It is also convenient that there is at least some criticism of the quintet. Settle's work has not yet received the full critical attention that the work of a number of her contemporaries has already gained, but there has been a beginning. And most attention has been directed at her major achievement—the quintet. Some distinguished novelists and critics have either reviewed the later books of the Beulah quintet as they appeared or have written essays about them. Two of these essays are of particular interest and value. The first, written by critic and book reviewer Granville Hicks, appeared as the foreword to the Ballantine paperback edition of *O Beulah Land*, published in August of 1965, the year when Ballantine brought out mass market paperback editions of what was identified at the time as the Beulah Land trilogy. In his foreword Hicks acknowledges the aid and comfort of another well-known critic and editor, Malcolm Cowley, who had first called Settle's work to his attention.

Hicks offers an accurate and helpful summary of the action and implications of the three books and some of the relationships among the characters of several generations. He is, appropriately, especially concerned with the first volume:

O Beulah Land is a remarkably realistic account of frontier

THE BEULAH QUINTET

life, which has so often been romanticized. Out of a close
familiarity with contemporary documents, Miss Settle has
won a deep insight into the ways in which her ancestors
lived and felt and thought. It is also a story of many strug-
gles, the struggle of man against nature, of white man
against Indian, of frontier adventurer against eastern gentle-
men. We meet many kinds of men and many kinds of
women, from the heroic Hannah to spoiled Sal Lacey, and
these people, good and bad, strong and weak, conquer the
land.[1]

In fact this is the main theme, and story conflict, which
Hicks discerned in the trilogy, "the relationship between land and people," which he described as "infi-
nitely complicated." Limiting his view to that theme and
subject, he found himself compelled to define Settle's
special place, her originality within the American tradition, as in opposition to the more familiar story of
"western migration." "But, although the westward
thrust is of vital importance in both history and legend,"
he writes, "the story has another side: There were
people who went so far and no farther, who made their
homes for generations in Boston or Richmond, in Buf-
falo or Pittsburgh. In her trilogy, of which *O Beulah Land*
is the first volume, Mary Lee Settle writes about the
families that settled in what is now West Virginia, and
she carries their story from the earliest pioneer days to
the present, telling what the land did to them and they
to the land." Certainly Hicks was correct in seeing that
the story of the land itself is at the center of the trilogy,
but by focusing so tightly on that single subject he

seems to have missed other significant threads which inform the overall story. Oddly, for Hicks had an earned reputation as a "political" critic, he appears to have missed some of the strong political themes and conflicts which fuel the novels. Perhaps the fact that Hicks, and other reviewers at the time, did not fully grasp the author's intentions helped persuade Settle that a trilogy was not enough, that she was not yet done with her story.

In any case Hicks's comments, while useful concerning the individual books and valuable in suggesting some of the qualities joining them together, have been superseded, at least in terms of the work as a whole, by the change and development of trilogy into quintet and by the revision of the final volume of the trilogy, *Fight Night on a Sweet Saturday*, which now survives only as a section, a part of the larger design of *The Killing Ground*. A second and more inclusive critical appreciation appeared in 1982 in the Ballantine paperback editions, serving as the introduction for all five volumes of what was by then known as the Beulah quintet. This piece was written by Robert Shattuck, critic and scholar, himself a winner of the National Book Award for *Marcel Proust* (1975), Commonwealth Professor of the University of Virginia, and, as she writes in her essay for *Contemporary Authors Autobiography Series (1)*, her mentor and adviser at just the time she began work on *The Killing Ground*. Speaking of the influence of Shattuck, Settle writes: "Beyond the erudition he shares with me, he has the genius as a critic and reader to thrust his fist

THE BEULAH QUINTET

into the center of a book. He guided me as I finished the last volume of the Beulah Quintet. He read it in all its drafts. He pointed out what was missing. . . . He wrote the superb introduction to the paperback edition. He led me to Robert Giroux, the most distinguished editor and publisher in America."[2] With even more specificity, in conversation, she has offered examples of Shattuck's critical counsel: "When I sent Roger the first draft of it to read, he said: 'You need a big scene like the scene in *Madame Bovary* at the farm auction.' He said, 'You need a big production number.' And so he sparked me into seeing the beginning of that book."

Shattuck's introduction, to which any future critics of the quintet will be required to return often and continue to consider, picks up the story of the land, which Hicks found central; but Shattuck sees it more as "a myth of the land" and is concerned to stress the epic and mythopoeic vision of the quintet: "The pivotal events around which her story takes shape are ritual, almost primordial happenings: feats, public ceremonials, formal balls, marriages, battles, violent deaths, funerals, and even mysterious descents far underground into the darkest entrails of the earth. The crucial scenes of the series give mythic scope to the classic American pioneer story."[3] Shattuck's essay, while in no way denying the sociopolitical elements deeply embedded in the quintet, serves to emphasize its larger and deeper implications and its place in world literature as something more, above and beyond the familiar ele-

UNDERSTANDING MARY LEE SETTLE

ments of the genre of "historical fiction" and the limits of regional writing.

It is interesting that the most extensive recent survey and study of the Beulah quintet is a mixed appreciation at best, often highly critical of aspects of the series. William J. Schafer's essay is, despite its stance of negative criticism, a useful examination, for the critic is chiefly at odds with the author on the levels of primary assumptions and intentions.[4] He argues that, in order to write the books of the quintet and to deal adequately with her "grand theme," which he defines as "the search for justice in a flawed world," she should have begun from a different set of assumptions about historical truth and should have employed different ways and means of telling her stories, something (both original assumptions and practical elements of storytelling) he sees to be intricately related. It is a complex argument, built mainly on his own assumption that historical truth is inevitably distorted when contained in "an individualistic-existential point of view." And he adds that the methods of the contemporary novel, her own use of which he highly praises in other works like *Blood Tie*, are wedded to that point of view and lead to "fragmentation and stasis," adequate for contemporary experience but not for a fully dimensional realization of historical fiction, and resulting in "twentieth century sensibilities trapped in a strange costume drama." There can be no real reply to his particular charges, since they derive from what might be called a critical intentional fallacy; that is, Settle should have intended to do something other than she did. But having allowed that there can be no meeting of minds on Schafer's broad and general assumptions, it remains to be said that his essay also offers useful insights into positive aspects of the quintet.

As to the criticism that her own assumptions and methods lead to the presentation of "twentieth century sensibilities trapped in a strange costume drama," it is important to be aware that Settle seems to have been concerned with this complex problem from the beginning of the creation of the series. In her interviews and in her major piece for the *New York Times Book Review*, "Recapturing the Past in Fiction,"[5] she has consistently stressed the importance of where and when she worked on a particular book. And to what purpose; that is, what present problems does her fiction, her imaginative investigation and re-creation of the past, address? For instance, her autobiographical memoir, a study of her own past, *All the Brave Promises* (1966), was at least partly inspired by events at the time of its creation (1964–1965) and the place she was living and working—Bard College, among the young. She has said in conversation: "The Vietnam War was escalating. So it seemed to me, in my impotent way, that the only thing I could do was to tell what it was really like in one small corner of the War [World War II]."

Or, as another example, she has indicated that she came to write *Prisons* at least partly out of her intellectual and emotional reactions to the 1960s, "the most profound psychic revolution this country ever had,"[6] and particularly her response to the violence and social chaos of the election year of 1968. She moved to London. She was thinking of the pattern of revolution turning to authoritarian dictatorship. So she studied and pondered, among other things, the English revolution and the times of Cromwell. "Somewhere in the past I was looking for the seed which would grow into our democracy," she writes, "for the books I had written about our past had not yet answered the question."[7] At Burford, in the Cotswolds, she found a stone wall in a churchyard where two soldiers had been executed by a firing squad in 1649, and there discovered an image and action to bring to life her troubling, still-abstract concept of her subject. She did a year of research and looking for the language to fit her characters and subject. She wrote the book on the Greek island of Kos and in Bodrum in Turkey in 1972. For some of the things happening around her then and there one can read *Blood Tie*, written later in America. At the time, she writes, "my inner landscape was in an English town in 1649."[8] Research, and especially the discovery of an appropriate language, set these imaginary people in the outer landscape of their given historical period. But the inner landscape, as evidenced by her use of allusions and parallels to the models of ancient myths, is a bringing together and blending of past and present. And as far as Settle is concerned, it can be, in honesty, no other way. Discussing the likenesses and the differences between the historian and the novelist, she is quite clear in her assumption that where we stand, at any given time and

THE BEULAH QUINTET

place in the present, profoundly informs what we are bearing witness to: "Historians find facts and shape theories; novelists find facts and make fiction. We both see from where we stand, and build from what we choose out of the protean past. History seeks inevitabilities. Fiction grows out of a doubt that may breed another kind of human understanding, drawn from the past, essential to the present."[9]

Making the Beulah Quintet

There is another kind of duality which exists for Settle and which must be joined together at the genesis of any book. She has described one of these two elements as concept, a more or less abstract subject, an intellectual curiosity. Image, on the other hand, is physical, sensual, and usually a mysterious presence, a flash of something happening. Image is essential. The concept or idea, she has said, "is like an unfertilized egg until it is fertilized with an image."[10] Already by the time *Kiss of Kin* (1955) was published, Settle had arrived at a concept and an image for her next work. "And in a curious way," she says, "this time the image came before the concept. The concept was a kind of questioning of the image." There were two images. "One was rejected and one wouldn't leave my head." The one that was rejected was of a couple in a car arguing. They were stuck, briefly, at the site of some road construction on the way to a mountain resort. "As I listened to them, the imagination of their argument, I wondered what was behind their arguing? What was between them? What was culture? That image didn't last, but the next one did. And that was of one man hitting another man in a drunk tank on a Saturday night. The concept came out of the questioning of the image. And that was: What is behind the fist of a man who hits a stranger? What is it? He doesn't know him. Why this stranger and not that stranger? Why? What is cultural? What is prejudice? What is background? I kept questioning and questioning and nothing went down on paper until I went back to an image. And the image was of a woman lost in the Endless Mountains."

It is this image, of Hannah Bridewell lost in the panic of flight, which becomes the prologue to *O Beulah Land* (1956). In her autobiographical essay for *Contemporary Authors Autobiography Series* and in "Recapturing the Past in Fiction," Settle has given some interesting and sometimes amusing details of the kinds of research she did to establish, for herself first of all, the authenticity and authority to re-create an eighteenth-century virgin American wilderness. "The sight of two bears across the New River in 'O Beulah Land' was measured by pacing the long, book-lined room (the North Library of the British Museum) and then watching the other end, waiting for a bear-sized human to pass to find out how much Hannah would have seen at that distance." Later she went to the London zoo: "The bear-keeper allowed me to go into the bear pit. I was armed with a can of Lyle's Golden Syrup. . . . I wanted to feel bears, and I did. Their fur was as stiff as a toilet brush."[11] These are not atypical rituals of writers trying to summon up the past, though Settle's insistence on the primary level of physical and sensuous authenticity, her demand of herself for the maximum possible physical accuracy, is unusual enough to place her among the few serious historical novelists.

But there was a more important quest, a different kind of knowledge required, before she could begin to write *O Beulah Land*. She has noted that people have a much larger "historic memory" than they realize, because, even with serious subjective distortions, it extends from recollections of early childhood back through the recollections and stories of old people, sometimes very old, in family circles—what she calls "a kind of folk memory." But it did not go back far enough to help her much with *O Beulah Land*. The physical world was more or less there because it was the world of her childhood in West Virginia, altered but accessible to imagination. But more was needed. "How and when it happened," she says, "was in the gold mine of the British Museum. . . . I realized that I had to construct a memory. And, like a primitive whose memory goes back a long way because they can't write—they write nothing down; they can't write something down and then forget it and look for it later—I sat in the British Museum and I read only contemporary works for about ten months until I had literally constructed a memory of language and events, everything, of the eighteenth century up to 1773."[12]

UNDERSTANDING MARY LEE SETTLE

Know Nothing came next, written mostly in America. And the concept was, in her words:

Why, within a hundred years of the genesis, was there a family decadence and a kind of not cynicism, but irony which had crept into the culture? And not only an irony, but a misplacement of historic memory, romanticizing of the past, a kind of psychic block to what had gone before. And I realized that what I was trying to do was become contemporary with people who either misremembered the past or didn't remember it at all, and at the same time, as a writer, to *know* the past. . . . I felt I was never going to get the image. Because what I was trying to find out was no less than the causes, within families, of the Civil War.

She describes herself as waiting and waiting for the arrival of the image. Finally she found it when she took her son and his friend into the mountains to go fishing and to have a picnic. Relaxing by the mountain stream, she had a sudden vision of a little boy being thrown into a river to learn how to swim. "That little boy was to grow up into Johnny Catlett."

"After *Know Nothing*," she says, "I made a very bad mistake. I thought by that time I was ready to write the book where the man hit the other man in the drunk tank. In a way it was my *Stephen Hero*, a first attempt to come back to the modern world." Believing that this story properly began early in the twentieth century in the coal fields, she wrote the first part based on a play called "Strike Night," which she recalls as something she wrote in the early 1950s. "It was about the daughter scripts. I did everything that fall to try and get some money together." She moved to England. In writing the book about the Scopes trial, she had done a chapter on the American Civil Liberties Union. "And I found the motto of the American Civil Liberties Union which was from a speech made by Jack Lilburne in the Star Chamber in the early 1630's. It begins: 'For what is done to any one may be done to every one. . . .' And it began to spark not an idea but a curiosity." Starting from Lilburne's speech and, she insists, without conscious purpose beyond the satisfaction of her curiosity, she began to study the period, its language, and particularly the ideas and the language of democracy. "And I began to realize that the trilogy wasn't a failure. It was incomplete. And part of its incompleteness had to do with the past. The eighteenth century was already late in our conceptual history. So the beginning of *Prisons* was a search rather than a concept. . . . As I got deeper into it the ideas came thick and fast; even though it was still conceptual, I think it was beginning already to form into a novel in an entirely new way for me. Because this was a search like a detective search." She was wondering whether in our Anglo-American history there had been, in Trotsky's terminology, a "time of the Thermidore," that moment when revolution has spent itself and turns back on itself, devouring with authoritarian reaction. Trotsky had cited the story of Napoleon and the French Revolution and his own story with Stalin. "Of course I found that exactly the same thing had happened in England with Cromwell's takeover, that Cromwell had

THE BEULAH QUINTET

taken over from the Left of the Parliamentary Army and the Levelers. I still had not found my story, but I was getting very concerned with its immediacy as a background to *O Beulah Land*."

With some friends she was visiting the Cotswolds and went to the small and beautiful old Oxfordshire village of Burford, set on the river Windrush. At the Norman Church of St. John the Baptist she was walking in the churchyard and found in the churchyard wall two lines of bullet holes, one line at about head level, the other above it. "I realized at once," she wrote, "that someone had been executed by a firing squad that was loath to do it." As she puts it in later conversation: "I simply walked into the churchyard and into the story of Johnny Church and Thankful Perkins." That, then, gave her "a direction in images and in language." To find out why this had happened and to understand it, she began her research and her attempt to submerge herself in the language of the period, not only from documents, but as much as possible from "the language of court cases or of contemporary popular plays, political debates, speeches, broadsheets quickly written and flung out overnight without any attempt at accepted educated style."[13] She even found an Oxford student with the regional accent of Cromwell's home county and got him to tape record some of Cromwell's speeches so that she could gain some clues as to cadence. "It has always astonished me, with the difficulty of finding the language, with becoming contemporary, which you have to do in a historical novel, so-called, because if you don't become that immediate with it, you don't have the empathy, that I ended up writing what is psychically the most autobiographical novel I have ever written. I guess there's something in me that still mourns for Johnny Church because . . . Johnny died without knowing that it's out of people who think they have failed that future success is written."

With the writing of *Prisons*, the trilogy had grown into four books. "And, of course, the great missing part was the mine wars." She mentions having found in the West Virginia State Library a 5,000-page transcript of the Senate investigation in 1913 of the Cherry Grove Massacre. All that information could now be combined with more personal recollection. "My mother and her sisters were girls in 1912. By now historic memory was getting to be personal memory. In a way I already knew the language. So I began to find *The Scapegoat*." The image which came to her was of the Gatling gun on the front porch of a house, as it appears in the opening paragraphs of *The Scapegoat*. "What are three pretty girls in white and a Gatling gun doing on the front porch of what looks like a house in the country?"

What had happened between the writing and publication of *Prisons* (1973) and the creation of *The Scapegoat* (1980) was the publication of *Blood Tie* (1977) and the subsequent liberating and reenergizing impact of public recognition, finally, in the form of the National Book Award. *The Scapegoat* was written in Charlottesville in the fall of 1976 and the spring of 1977. "In the fall of 1977 I went to Italy because I found that I knew no past for epigraph from *The Revolution Betrayed* by Leon Trotsky) and a short "Afterword." These elements are more than decorative, and Settle was deeply annoyed when the British version of the novel, *The Long Road to Paradise*, was published without the "Foreword" and with the "Afterword" acting as a prologue. The "Foreword," which also serves as the foreword for the whole quintet, is expository and informational, a concise and well-executed piece of historical writing presenting the background and context of the English Revolution in the 1640s, briefly introducing the principal historical figures, ending with a one-paragraph account of the "one new leader" to come out of the wars, "Oliver Cromwell, a minor member of Parliament from the fen country, honed on the battlefield, who had proved himself a brilliant natural soldier." The brisk "Afterword" begins with a contemporary journalistic account of the execution of Johnny Church and the others and a brief expository account of what became of some of the chief surviving characters, real and imaginary. It is the latter who get the last lines, pushing the story on toward *O Beulah Land*. Beyond the value of "Foreword" and "Afterword" in furnishing enough historical fact to "place" the story for the reader whose detailed knowledge is sketchy, these sections have a larger function. For, set as the first and last word of *Prisons*, they help by ironic contrast to vivify the fiction of Johnny Church's narrative. One can see by demonstration how conventional historical prose, based upon fact and abstraction, is wholly inadequate to contain the story of this young

THE BEULAH QUINTET

man. And yet, also by this demonstration, that is in truth the case. Church's vivid, living and breathing (and dying) story comes, in the present, out of plain factual history. And in the end his story fades first into journalism and then into further exposition. So that one of the things which Settle is showing, essential to her subject and the themes of the quintet, is how history, when it is accurate, is always based on what happened in the lives of people, known and unknown, of flesh and blood. That it is the *imagined* characters (not imaginary; for their names, at least, were known) who live most fully in *Prisons* makes another complex comment on the inadequacy of conventionally abstract, factual discourse to re-create very much reality.

Once past the establishing exposition of the "Foreword," the reader is at once plunged into the narrative account, in first person, of the life of the protagonist—Jonathan Church. First-person storytelling offers several strong advantages at this point. It allows for a voice, and a language for that voice to use, to be efficiently and directly established. And first-person narration offers some traditional strengths. Authenticity is one of these. To overcome the contemporary reader's ignorance of the past, particularly this confused and partly forgotten part of history, there is nothing more instantly immediate than a speaker from the time who is fully alive as an imaginary character. Witnesses and narrators are trusted, in fiction at least, until they definitively prove themselves to be unreliable or, at any rate, severely limited. The farther removed in time, space, or common

reality, the more important the character of the reporting witness becomes. Which is why so many stories of
fantasy and ghost stories, for example, avail themselves
of the powers of first-person narration. Johnny Church
was credibility and authority. He is acutely sensitive, all
five senses adroitly evoked by the author so that what
happens to him is "real" in the sense that a body, flesh
and blood, enjoys or endures it all. By the same token
his voice, in the language Settle has created to echo the
language of his times, works in two ways. First, by its
distinct difference from our own written and spoken
language it establishes a certain distance between the
reader and the narrator and other people and the events
of the time, making them all, at first and appropriately,
somewhat alien. Alien and mildly exotic they may be,
but must never be merely quaint; for that would diminish everything. Meantime the substance, the events and
memories, though they may be in details different from
contemporary experience, must also seem to be part of
the shared and universal pulse of things. And the
sensory affective experience must become powerfully
immediate. Then, gradually, as readers accustom themselves to the rhythms and habits of the language, as in
a foreign language composed of close cognates, it becomes more and more familiar, thus more transparent.
What is happening, then, is that readers are having
experiences and developing memories out of this material. To support this, Jonathan's story begins in the
present tense as he rides in the rear guard of the
Parliamentary army, together with his close friend

THE BEULAH QUINTET

Thankful Perkins, half asleep, nodding, remembering. He remembers his own childhood in vivid images (and in a contrasting past tense). One comes to know him and his times through his memories as much as his present experiences.

All of this works well and strongly in the isolated context of *Prisons*, as a single novel in and of itself. But in the larger sense of the whole design it is urgently important that this, the very first voice, offer an even stronger memory pattern which will haunt all five books and all of the characters in them, though they, unlike readers, can never be consciously aware of the ghosts, ideas and images as well as people with voices, who haunt them.

Essentially the story he tells of himself is how he grew up in a strict Puritanical household, strongly in contrast to the household of Lacy House, ruled over by his uncle, Sir Valentine Lacy, and Nell Cockburn Lacy, his aunt. His own father, who began life as a poor apprentice "to a tallow chandler in Cheapside," made himself wealthy enough to be newly among the gentry. At twenty, looking back, Jonathan Church sees that his father used his wounds and scars to make himself rich: "I saw him climb and claw his way up some Jacob's ladder of advancement until he was a country man and owned land, all enclosed, heart and all. He was goaded by his own hunger, by cold, and by a strange and ever-present conviction that he was born too late."[14] Johnny Church is torn between his own limited understanding and vision of his father's house, Henlow, built upon an ancient ruin, and Lacy House only six miles away. He grew up; the wars began and took place around him, involving his father on the Parliamentary side. He went at fourteen to Oxford, where he clashed with cruel Cavalier fellows and was whipped for "new-fangled democratical notions." "Democratical was the most evil word at Oxford when the king was there, and little better after" (60). It was at Oxford that he came to know of Lilburne and began to imagine the possibility of changing the world for the better:

> If the king's fanfarons aped him, my dear friends and I aped Freeborn Jack Lilburne as shamelessly. Why, it was like a dawn breaking for me to hear all that martyr's words, unspoken even in my wildest thoughts before, and now printed and hid beneath my pillow, to be learned with more zeal than all the dusty mumblings from tutors' mouths. We kept, my friends and I, many a late vigil over these new things and thought to change the world (61).

Called home to Henlow as the situation deteriorated in England, Johnny elected on his sixteenth birthday to rebel against his father over a particular act of insensitive cruelty. He went off to Lacy House, where he discovered Sir Valentine dying (and with him the old England of the old country aristocracy). He was, without difficulty and no shame at the time, seduced by his aunt. Outfitted with money and equipment from the Lacys, who honored his conscience ("Kin and neighbors are a damn sight closer than politics," Sir Valentine had said), he rode off to find the wars. First he met the old

THE BEULAH QUINTET

soldier Gideon MacKarkle, "a ragged dynasty of a man," and finally joined Oliver Cromwell's forces.

Thereafter the story follows Church and his friends, Gideon and especially Thankful Perkins, a good and simple man of great faith, through his first major battle at Naseby—as fine a piece of writing of the first confused experience of combat, as felt and witnessed by a raw recruit, as any we have, including its great model, *The Red Badge of Courage.* To save his own life, he kills his first enemy with a poleax: "His blood ran down my coat, a gout of blood I still wear, faintly, after so long. That loosening ragged death after the urgency of his strong muscles, that body's giving up, as one after the pitch of love, was too foul to tell of, that awful second of the same satisfaction, the same" (95). And after that he is a veteran.

The gradual disintegration of the army follows— "We, who had been called the Saints, disintegrated into thieving, some into rioting, some to desertion, all into bitter, bitter disappointment" (105)—and the gradual triumph of authority, Cromwell, over conscience and idealism. The king was gone, in a single brisk paragraph. ("I fear the knees of slaves more than the gray ghost of the king" [130]). Then the crisis in Ireland and the refusal of so many of the "democratical" Parliamentary soldiers to go and serve there. Thankful writes: "What have we to do in Ireland, to fight and murder a people and nation who have done us no harm?" Thankful and Jonathan Church are elected Agitators for their regiments, an honorable, representative post, for which they must later suffer to intimidate the others. Cromwell will not negotiate with them ("Must I quarrel with every dog in the street that barks at me?" [180]). The last pages, leading up to the execution of Thankful and Johnny, are a great debate between authority and conscience. Johnny Church, being educated and from good family, is given a chance to live if he will use his influence with the disaffected to persuade them to follow their leader obediently. He makes the free and tragic choice of conscience and dies for it. And on that same evening of 17 May 1649, the reader learns in the "Afterword," Cromwell received an honorary degree, as a Doctor of Civil Law at Magdalen College. And also learns that Jonathan Church has left a son by his aunt, Jonathan Lacy, thought to be the last son of Sir Valentine, a son who "would have been typical of those young men who went to Virginia in the 1670's, for what was there in England to keep a young man there, born to ruin and living on cold charity?" (256).

Thus, in the first book of the series there is a clear outline of what the basic subject and basic themes of the quintet will be: that it will be an accounting of history in terms of the never-ending conflict between liberal conscience, the youthful dream of liberty, and the power of authority; that it will be played out in violence and on the edge of violence, but always in terms of family and kinship, of bloodlines, known and unknown; that what is good and true, exemplary, will be knowledge and understanding and the acceptance of duty; that those who are good and worthy, to one degree or another, are

THE BEULAH QUINTET

those "who quest, who wander, who question;"[15] that those who are wicked and unworthy (to one degree or another) are those who are cruel or overprivileged and too comfortable or too weak to hold to any serious beliefs. And together with family names and any number of image clusters which will recur in various patterns, linking the separate stories, there is the central classical myth which holds the whole quintet together— the story of Antigone and Creon. Ironically it is Cromwell (Creon) who causes the recollection, but Johnny Church, so recently an Oxford scholar, does the remembering:

"This I will do before my God. What else can I do?" Cromwell ends with that question. The trees turn their leaves slowly to a new breeze from up the Windrush, and there is nothing in me now but this moment so sweet so suddenly, so free 'tis like only the weight of singing. That is the question that Creon asked her, the girl with the dirt clutched in her fist; her uncle asked Antigone that final question, and she had no answer for him, for his words took place somewhere else, stars away from her, and so she turned her wrist and turns it still. . . . That's all that stands against their power to damn and diminish us, the turning of a wrist (192–93).

There are many classical allusions and parallels in the quintet, but the strongest single myth is the story of Antigone.

The next book of the series, *O Beulah Land*, is set a full century later in time; located, at least at the outset, in the wilderness of the new continent; already in another kind of English language, changed through time and by the natural reticence and the lack of education of most of the characters. It is a tale with a very different method of storytelling—a third-person, omniscient, chiefly scenic and dramatic narration, a kind of narration that is ideal to focus concentration, with considerable objectivity, on events. Much happens and sometimes very quickly. It is, then, a large tale; the cast of important, principal characters is large, and their interconnections are complex. And the time scheme, rather than being the kind of straightforward chronology of a few deeply intense days in the middle of May in 1649, enriched and enlarged by the personal memories of a single protagonist, Jonathan Church, is a full twenty years, almost generational. In fact, Hannah Bridewell and Jeremiah Catlett, the first people met in the "Prologue" (Hannah is almost nineteen at the time) and who die violently in the last sequence, an Indian attack, leave behind a son, Ezekiel, who is almost as old as Hannah had been at the beginning. A full lifetime has fallen in between.

The tone of the whole book is determined and dominated by its "Prologue," four short chapters and roughly fifty pages of virtuoso writing around the theme of survival against enormous odds. It begins with a high, distant, almost abstract (except that the language is wonderfully concrete) view of a woman lost and alone in the wilderness, "a haunted, chased creature mindless with panic" and "kept alive only by some boundless

THE BEULAH QUINTET

miracle that lets the nervous fawns live, or the silly, vulnerable fish."[16] "I saw her stripped down to nothing," Settle has said in conversation, "but life and survival. She had no memory. She had a direction and that was all. Because what I realized that I was doing was tracing the genesis of our being in this country. And instead of trying to write social history, I was putting it in terms of single people. A woman was lost in the Endless Mountains, and I wanted the reader and myself to experience the pure luxury of having *any* kind of food and *any* kind of shelter."

In terms of single people. The narrator circles and observes, then suddenly comes down and joins Hannah physically in her hunger, her bone-weariness, her panic, as she survives her forty days and forty nights in the wilderness. Most of the allusions and parallels here are biblical, for the characters, even the illiterate ones, know their scripture. And it is in scriptural terms that they see their experience having meaning, making any sense. The reader follows her reduction to the purity of a surviving (barely so) animal. And there comes this moment when, sleeping in a cave to escape the chill rain, she finds she is not alone there: "But she woke, frozen, when she felt movement, felt the great, living, damp, soft pelt beside her, and knew that whatever beast it was, tired to death too, had crept close to her for her pathetic warmth, and still purred, drifting to sleep, meaning no harm" (21).

Much later—years later in the life of Hannah—readers will learn how she happened to be present, as were so many other characters in this story, at the crushing defeat of the army of British General Braddock, in July of 1755, by the French and Indians, near Fort Duquesne. How she was taken captive and held by the Indians. How she escaped to come here.

She is found and saved and slowly nursed back to health by Jeremiah Catlett, equally alone, living alone in a hut with his sow Hagar. As Hannah heals, she learns his story—how he was sold into indentured servitude from Liverpool at the age of five, suffered much, fell in with an itinerant preacher, was converted and ran away to be with him. And now he lives alone like a religious hermit until he is sorely tempted by the presence of the young woman, strong now, who lives with him. Alone in the woods he searches his memory and the scripture there for wisdom, the strength to overcome temptation. But he fails. "Unhappily, neither the heat, the desert, the luxury, nor the hard-bought imperial wisdom which brought forth the Ecclesiastes was there—only the cold words and the snow and a twenty-five-year-old man alone" (54).

Here then, in Settle's version, are America's Adam and Eve: Hannah Bridewell, who is a transported whore from London, and Jeremiah Catlett, fugitive indentured servant, coming together with a wordless animal passion in a dirt-floored hut in the Endless Mountains:

So when he did look at her, close to him, and smelled the sweet smell of her sweat of the morning, and the fresh crushed tobacco dust which still clung to her face and hair;

brilliant and overwhelming moment. No wonder that before *Prisons* became part of the background of this story, some readers and critics tended to lose sight of the basic and larger political theme. One aspect of social statement comes across emphatically, however. In later volumes the descendants of these earliest settlers will often have either forgotten the truth of where they come from, where and how it began, or, in the false lights and colors of the imagination, they will paint a beautified picture of the past, prettier, but far less vital and powerful. And, indeed, that is another strong thematic thread in the whole quintet—the power, for good and/or ill, of the imagination to transmute raw material into myth. The imagination can find and tell truth or lies. If the imagination settles for lies, the results, no matter how briefly comforting, will be severely crippling.

This effect is clearly shown in the story of other principal characters and especially in the sad times of Sally Lacey, far from the settled east and at a loss on the crude frontier. She is the wife (and great burden) to Jonathan Lacey, who is, unknowing, a direct descendant of Jonathan Church. Jonathan is a strong, positive character, a soldier and a planter and founder of the "dynasty" of Beulah. Like his ancestor, he has compassion and an open mind. Near the end of the novel he has just been elected by the others and sent off as their representative to Williamsburg ("You stand bluff for usn, Johnny. Stand bluff to the governor. Larn him how stubborn Virginians can git!") His daughter, Sara, marries Ezekiel Catlett. But his son, Perry (Peregrine), is a

THE BEULAH QUINTET

murderous psychopath and must be disinherited. And his poor sad, weak wife, Sally, never adjusts to the hard life of the frontier or allows her imagination, slowly tainted by misapprehensions, to accept very much reality. The seeds of what may follow are planted in *O Beulah Land*, though it ends with some hope for the future, if only with the hope of some of the most prescient characters—like the marvelously drawn Jarcey Pentacost, scholar and printer and free spirit—that the American Revolution is close at hand.

Know Nothing, jumping ahead almost another century of time, concerns among other things the coming on of the Civil War. It opens with the image Settle described, with (on 29 July 1837) the next Johnny, Johnny Catlett, being thrown by his father into the Great Kanawha river to sink or swim. He swims and, as if in tribal rite, is accepted by his father, Peregrine Lacey Catlett, master of Beulah. Who begins to tell him:

"God in his Providence saw fit to give your family bottom-land along the river, and put our people under our care." . . .

He liked the way Minna told him that better. She said, "Listen here, Marse Johnny, we owns this here valley. We owns the mose people, and the mose horses, and the mose cows, and the mose land. We ships the best salt and we got the mose plates and furniture. I knows, I done been a heap of places and seed. So don' you go actin like po whites ain't got nothin." That made him feel like the Knights of Old.[17]

Minna is accurate in her description of where Beulah

stands at the beginning of the story—a peak of seeming power and affluence, the land already radically changed from the hard wilderness Johnny's grandparents knew.

It is all contained there—the essential conflict, remaining to be outlined and developed through an elaborate sequence of events, large and small, in the lives of, again, a large crowd of characters, major and minor. One of the major reviews of *Know Nothing*, by William Peden for *Saturday Review*, while praising the novel highly, found the number and variety of characters to be a problem: "The plethora of weakly-individualized people, together with the author's fondness for caricature and her confusing use of a floating point of view, is the major weakness of Miss Settle's novel."[18] Basically this is a subjective critical complaint, but is mentioned here to stress that the size of the cast seemed relatively large and surprising even to a highly regarded professional writer and critic.

Know Nothing becomes primarily the story of the obligation, settled, at the outset and again in the final section, on Johnny Catlett as if it were his bounden duty, to protect and to defend, to *conserve* the already threatened way of life the inhabitants of Beulah Land have come to since the hard and perilous times of Hannah and Jeremiah. So much has happened in such a short time. The land has been taken and tamed for profit, but requires slaves to maintain it. Even the stories of the past have changed. Perry Lacey, the murderous and disinherited son of Jonathan Lacey, is now honored in memory as Colonel Peregrine Lacey, "this great Injun

THE BEULAH QUINTET

fighter and glorious hero of the Revolution, . . . an American hero and patriot" (51). And even the Catletts have acquired the patina of a false history:

"They came over to England with William the Conqueror. They were knights," Mrs. Catlett still went on. "The first Catlett came to Virginia because of religious persecution. My sister-in-law's niece found all this out. Let me see who she married. Sometimes I forget" (74).

The language has changed. Now there seems to be a firm separation, a dichotomy between the living speech spoken by Minna, a slave, and a more "literary" language which is at once romantic and nostalgic, based, Settle says, on the fiction of Walter Scott. Thinking in that language transmutes present reality into false myth, "Knights of Old." Johnny Catlett, at the beginning, is more than a little like Tom Sawyer. And the world of *O Beulah Land*, almost wholly forgotten by most of the principal characters, has turned upside down. In such a little time the women, who had mostly been hard survivors, equal sharers of the wilderness and the frontier, are turned into variations not on the original model of Hannah, but much more on the lines of the poor deluded Sally Lacey. They are at best decorative dependents; so much so that when Johnny's father dies, near the end of the story, he can, in dying advice, offer his son this counsel: "Be good to them. Poor innocent things. I've always taught you that, ain't I, Johnny? Women and niggers. They ain't fitten to look after theirselves" (269). The women of the family, including various unattached kinfolk, are trapped not only by the manners, habits, and circumstances of the times, but in the terms of a false myth. And the best of them are intelligent enough to know it and to resent it bitterly even as they patiently live out their own form of servitude. In what is, in fact, the longest sustained section in the book, the family goes to the resort spa at Egeria Springs (modeled on White Sulphur Springs) in an attempt to engage in the complex mating rituals of the times, hoping to find eligible husbands for the marriageable women. Here there is a fascinating picture of the clothing and the manners of the period.[19]

The story, told not in a "floating point of view" but rather, in the manner of *O Beulah Land*, in a straightforward, third-person, omniscient manner, moving within that freedom from one limited third-person point of view to another, is mainly centered around the young life of Johnny Catlett. He grows up into a tragic figure of quite different dimension, indeed almost opposite to his long-lost and long-forgotten true ancestor—Johnny Church—although he in fact shares much also, including some real courage, sensitivity, compassion, and finally the wisdom of self-knowledge. The story shows him growing up into manhood, shows him learning, at the University of Virginia, later in a hard life out West and in the terrible times in Kansas in 1856. He becomes someone, far from guiltless, but after all honorable and worthwhile; and, at the end, just as the Civil War is beginning, a war he knows, rationally, has doomed his

THE BEULAH QUINTET

side, his way of life, and is wrong and unjust, but in which he must serve, must kill and perhaps be killed, all out of a sense of familial duty, a living obligation freely, if wearily, undertaken and, finally, beyond right and wrong. Just at the end of things in this story, as he is surrounded by many names familiar to the quintet reader (there is even the latest Gideon McKarkle to take and to tend his horse), Johnny Catlett has a brief bright moment of pure witness: "As in other moments of his life, he knew complete stillness, the stillness of the woods, of sorrow, of night—just for a moment, acting on him. He knew it had begun and the luxury of questioning was over, thrown away" (334). And so he must step forward and do his duty, even as once Johnny Church had taken his last tragic step. But in a sense Catlett's action is sadder, more classically tragic in that this performance of his duty lacks even the assurance of good conscience. The one act of the martyrdom of conscience is performed by a minor character, a preacher named Charles McAndrews, who recognizes Johnny in Missouri and asks Johnny to carry the message to his mother in Virginia that he has gone to preach love and liberty in bloody Kansas. " 'Tell her I had no choice. Tell her'—he was trying to find the words—'I had to love my enemies. It was my tragedy that they were my own people.' " Johnny observes him: "He had the profile of a man who dreamed and called it thought, who in another time might have gone into politics when revolutionary men were listened to, or in another place might have been a poet" (253). And in a sense it is

McAndrews in this brief meeting who absolves him in advance, saying: "Perhaps you are the kind loyalty's more important to. Greater love hath no man. . . . A man like you caint live a heartless life" (254).

Johnny Catlett's last act before going out into the confusion of the first skirmish of the war is a brief prayer that says it all: " 'Oh God,' he prayed, 'forgive us our sins and don't let me have to kill my brother' " (334).

His brother is Lewis, a preacher and an abolitionist who is also cruel, obsessed, utterly uncharitable and abstracted from his own humanity. The reader can be sure, safe in the knowledge of what was to come to pass, that he will prove to be an implacable, indefatigable enemy.

Since the next volume of the quintet, *The Scapegoat*, leads into the twentieth century and a different sort of historical memory, it is important to pause here long enough to acknowledge what sort of history Settle created in the first three volumes of the series, what she has added or changed from the conventional view. *Prisons* surprises with its accurate and contemporary understanding of how early and how fully certain ideals now taken for granted were planted in the Anglo-American consciousness. It likewise revises conventional thinking about the revolutionary period of the middle seventeenth century. Much of that, a revolution within a revolution which ended with the Restoration, has been lost to Americans. *O Beulah Land*, in large part because of the accuracy and authenticity of its details,

THE BEULAH QUINTET

presents eighteenth-century, pre-Revolutionary America in a harder, tougher, more endangered time and place than many with hindsight have chosen to remember. There is something of vision she shares with the very different novelist Kenneth Roberts, but he wrote of Maine. The South had not been so accurately and starkly presented. With *Know Nothing*, while nothing there mitigates the crimes of the antebellum South, much serves to make the beginning of the Civil War as tragic for the region as it was for her character Johnny Catlett. The system and the society were dying from the inside, anyway, rotten at the core. But she has remarkably presented good men and true who were caught by conflicting forces larger than any man, as doomed as any dynastic figures in a Greek tragedy. In one sense *Know Nothing* might be seen in part as Creon's side of the story.

The Scapegoat tells the story, from various angles and in several styles, of the beginning of a coal strike in West Virginia (Beulah Land was still a part of Virginia in *Know Nothing*) in 1912. Tightly plotted, and complex in its own terms as well as in relation to the rest of the quintet, *The Scapegoat* is a large novel, not a *long* novel, without sprawl or prolixity. Its cast of characters is both extensive and various, ranging from mine owners to native mountaineers and coal miners, from an English geologist and a Scottish engineer to the immigrant families newly arrived to dig out the coal. There are "ladies" and mountain women, and there is a wonderful rendering of an amazing historical figure, the union organizer Mother Jones. People of all ages are treated and developed sympathetically.

Much has changed since the old plantation days. King Coal has created the greatest changes. And nowdays the Laceys are in the coal business. There is the father, Beverley Lacey, a weak but kindly and well-meaning man, mine owner; his religious wife, Ann Eldridge Lacey; and their three daughters (in order): Lily, Althea, and Mary Rose. The latest Catlett, Jake, though kinfolk, is head of the local union. There is the violent and dangerous Captain Daniel Chester Neil (descended from Big Dan O'Neill of *Know Nothing*), who will later marry Althea. There are, among the immigrants, the Paganos—Annunziata, the matriarch, and her handsome son, Eddie (Eduardo), who is as it happens a friend of Lily Lacey. It is a friendship that will save his life even as it costs someone else (the scapegoat—Carlo Michele) his own.

For this novel Settle has noted moving into the zone of her own historic memory. Her mother and aunts were alive in 1912. They carried the language of their childhood with them. She had heard it all her life. Moreover there were more commonplace things than family treasures, antiques and relics to touch and use. Settle says that she found real clothes for Lily, clothes she could have worn. And she used to ask close friends, including writer Ann Beattie, to put on "Lily's" clothes so that she could see how they looked on someone sitting, standing, moving. The research, including trial

THE BEULAH QUINTET

transcripts of the period and talks with people who had seen Mother Jones in fact and flesh, was easier and more assured. And, part of the ease and assurance behind the whole book, it should be remembered that she began to put *The Scapegoat* together in the confident awareness that at last, at the age of 60 with *Blood Tie*, she had been recognized and had earned for herself a place at the high table of the literary establishment.

The Scapegoat has some surprises for the reader who has followed the quintet from its beginning. There is the matter of primary narrative time. *O Beulah Land* covers twenty years, 1754–1774. *Know Nothing* deals with 1837–1861. And while it is true that the main line of action of *Prisons*, at least in the central narrative of Johnny Church, is confined to a few days (12–17 May 1649), the character of the first-person narration is to create an immediacy and freedom in time well beyond the imposed limits of "actual" time. The time of any first-person story is all present and simultaneous, the time of the telling. Told in four precisely timed and identified sections, *The Scapegoat* begins at 3:00 p.m. on Friday, 7 June 1912 and ends at 8:00 a.m. on Saturday, 8 June 1912. There is a good deal of freedom within the boundaries of this apparently strict time scheme. There are gracefully executed background exposition and personal memories, seeming to derive naturally out of present action and reaction in the story. For example, there is the necessary Italian, old-country background of the Pagano family, originally from Perugia. Much more unusual, however—and in fact daring in surprising audacity—are Settle's use of flash forwards in time, presenting action that will take place later as part of the line of this story. For example, section 3 begins with a monologue by the middle sister, Ann Althea Lacey, now married to a central character in the primary story, Daniel Chester Neill, mine detective, a little drunk at this telling and, as is discovered in a swift, one-sentence aside, fifteen years older than the Althea of the story. As a witness of events Althea has some justifiable confidence in herself: "I can tell what happened better drunk than the rest of them can sober. . . . Hell yes. Dreams and gin are no respecters of time."[20] Similarly the reader learns what will happen (in the past tense, as if it had already happened, which, in truth, for the reader after 1980, it has) to Lily Ellen Lacey, who comes closest to playing the central role of protagonist in this novel. Asked where the "Johnny" character of *The Scapegoat* is to be found—the protean character, Johnny Church, Jonathan Lacey, Johnny Catlett, Settle replied "Johnny is Lily." Lily, eldest of the three Lacey daughters of this generation, after the events contained in this novel goes first to England, then to France in May of 1916 as a nurse in a Voluntary Aid Detachment, "posted to France, to Voisincourt on the river Ancre"; and there she bears witness to some of the most terrible slaughter of this bloody century.

One of the values gained from this surprising introduction of future time within the context of present, forward-moving time in this story is another perspective on the events of the story. *The Scapegoat* is,

THE BEULAH QUINTET

on the basic narrative level, held together by the suspense generated by the coming of the 1912 coal strike with its considerable potential for violence and personal tragedy. There are moments of real sorrow, and violence claims the life of one innocent man, the "scapegoat" of the title. But even the worst of the violence in West Virginia, potential as well as realized, fades into puny insignificance measured against the incredible fire storm of violence to come. There is a huge difference. And yet there is a real connection also. After all, the genesis of the story began in the author's mind, and likewise begins as a narrative, with a Gatling gun, a machine gun, incongruous and menacing, shiny and unloaded, on the front porch of the Lacey house. That particular gun causes no damage here. A few years later Lily must deal with the results of the military use of this relatively new weapon—the machine gun. Among other things it kills young Englishman Neville Roundtree, who figured in the events of 1912 as an agent and employee of the absentee English mine owners. Writing to her mother, trying to tell her what it is like (in the end she tears up her own letter hopelessly), Lily says:

"The slaughter has been huge. They say fifty thousand casualties the first day. There isn't enough of anything. Men are on the beds and there are stretchers under them with more men. . . . I found some wounded from the 8th Devons who could tell me about Mr. Roundtree. He was killed at Mansel Copse by machine gun fire. They say over a hundred and fifty men were killed by one machine gun. They were all buried together in one trench. They put a wooden notice over it. 'The Devonshires held this trench. The Devonshires hold it still.' " She wanted to write, "That's what a machine gun does, Mother," and then, "I want to come home," but she didn't let herself do that, or cry anymore (170).

This is an almost Chekovian plotting. As a matter of fact Chekov appropriately haunts this story. In an interview, talking of *The Scapegoat*, Settle has said: "What if Chekov had written *The Three Sisters* and set it right in the middle of the October Revolution?"[21]

Another technical surprise in *The Scapegoat*, another example of an audacious confidence and authority, is the way Settle uses point of view to tell her story. Considering the expository narrative, the "Foreword" and "Afterword" which bracket Jonathan Church's first-person story in *Prisons*, her method had always been fully omniscient. But in *The Scapegoat* she carries the power of that strategy to a new level. Just as within the stated time frame she allows herself great freedom, so here she shifts rapidly and deftly in and out of first-person and third-person narration, giving herself the opportunity and occasion to shift and blend language, often on the same page, sometimes in the same paragraph (for a *character*, in the first-person mode, may shift into a limited third-person accounting of actions witnessed or imagined), the language of speech and the written language. This allows every principal character at least two kinds of language, written and spoken, simultaneously; at the same time, paradoxically, it puts

THE BEULAH QUINTET

the author, hand in glove with the reader, in total control. Settle points the camera where she chooses when she is ready, turns on or off the sound system as she pleases.

The proof of the virtuosity of *The Scapegoat* lies in the fact that the prominent and distinguished critics who became a little choir of praise for the novel (as if to make up, if they could, for the years of neglect) saw that it worked splendidly, but seemed unaware of *how* it worked, of how unusual her storytelling method really was. Robert Houston came closest in his essay review for *The Nation*, describing the novel as "a symphony of her characters' voices, captured with an unfailingly attuned ear."[22] Novelist Anne Tyler had nothing but praise for the book in her *Washington Post* review: "It's a whole slice of a long-ago world with leaves still rustling and its voices still murmuring—a quiet masterpiece."[23] And E. L. Doctorow was equally enthusiastic in his front-page review for the *New York Times Book Review*.[24] Jonathan Yardley (who would turn against her next novel, *The Killing Ground*) was among those who honored her and, inadvertently perhaps, honored her magical technique by not noticing it: "Settle writes clean, spare prose. It is also beautiful prose, but it does not call attention to itself."[25] In his introduction for the Ballantine paperback editions of the Beulah quintet Roger Shattuck has compared and contrasted her use of time and point of view with the techniques of William Faulkner. He sees them as equally complex but different. Settle's use of time and point of view is deliberately more accessible to the engaged reader. It also makes a slightly different statement about the possibility of imaginative understanding:

His [Faulkner's] characters spend their lives circling around it in exhausting, sometimes spectacular loops that constantly breed further loops of memory and speculation. In the Beulah Quintet, Miss Settle's narrative loops—rarely so compulsive or so extravagant as Faulkner's—establish a distance and a perspective from which the action can at intervals return to the straightaway of experience. True being is not timeless. Rather we come upon it when the stream of individual consciousness coincides briefly with the stream of time shared with others. . . . After long preparation and many missed turns, a perceptive individual may participate fully in a recognizable event of genuine significance to him and to others. It is a rare accomplishment in modern fiction.[26]

With *The Scapegoat*, Settle and her series of novels had at last arrived. It remained to see how she would transform *Fight Night on a Sweet Saturday* and bring the quintet to a close.

In the beginning of section 2 of *The Killing Ground* Hannah McKarkle says this: "Thankful Perkins had called the road I was traveling the long road to Paradise. If his road had ended in the genes of people in Beulah valley, for me it had begun there, too. I had, at last, to go back to the event, the act that had begun my search, the fury of one unknown fist hitting an unknown face."[27]

THE BEULAH QUINTET

In the creation of *The Killing Ground*, Settle chose to develop a surprising (astonishing would not be too strong a word) narrative strategy. She wanted, of course, to revise and to retell the story of the death of Johnny McKarkle in the drunk tank following the Labor Day dance of 1960 and the quest of his sister, Hannah, to find how it had happened and somehow to lay his restless spirit to rest. It had been what the whole sequence of books had pointed toward since she began *O Beulah Land* in about 1954. And this story had been previously completed, albeit in edited and truncated form, in *Fight Night on a Sweet Saturday* (1964). There had been the addition of two full-length books, *Prisons* and *The Scapegoat*, to the series, and there had been twenty years of contemporary history, some of which—especially the later 1960s, after the death of the fictional Johnny McKarkle and after the completion and publication of *Fight Night on a Sweet Saturday*—had, in her view, radically changed the psychic climate of America. Already *Fight Night* was historical, a full generation behind herself and the times. There had been, she believed, another revolution. Perhaps it was now again the age of the Thermidore. But in any case the earlier novel was conceived by her as inadequate. She had to find a way, a story of something larger, with more apt contemporaneity into which the story of Johnny McKarkle could be incorporated, still central, crucial, but more intricately related to past and future than it had ever been. Whatever the new book, new version or vision, would be, it must do two things at once—stand as a single story in

UNDERSTANDING MARY LEE SETTLE

and of itself, at least on one level, a level Settle has described in conversation as "without the irony"; and at the same time it must do something to bring the whole series to a natural, acceptable, and credible conclusion.

What Settle chose to do, a daring and risky choice yet wonderfully efficient, was to make Hannah McKarkle a writer like herself. And something more. Not any writer, but the author of the four previous novels of the Beulah quintet, by name and title. In the opening section, "The Return: June 1978," Hannah has been asked back to Canona to help at a fund-raiser by giving a lecture. The book opens with someone musing about the prehistoric, three-thousand-year-old archaeology of the region, the bones of seven-foot giants found in an ancient burial/killing ground. And she easily refers to Johnny Church, to Lily, to the Hannah of *O Beulah Land*, and others from the quintet. She also summons up the dominant classical myth which informs the quintet: "I know, if anyone does, why Antigone had to bury the evasive Polynices. She buried an obsession so it would not haunt her. She had to bless him who was unblessed. At last, at last, she must have told herself, grief-stricken and relieved, I will know where he is" (13). Soon enough she is being introduced to her audience: "Uh, she is the author of numerous works of fiction including *Prison* I mean *Prisons O Beulah Land Know Nothing*. She is working on a novel about the coal business in 1912 called *The Scapegoat*" (39).

Just as there is throughout the quintet a subtle and reciprocal relationship between fact—historical, politi-

THE BEULAH QUINTET

cal, geographical, social, and personal—and fiction, so the creation of the fictional character Hannah McKarkle at once supported and justified Settle's relationship with her own fiction. But there were simpler and more practical reasons and values for this overt transmutation. For one thing, she wanted Hannah to be younger than herself, to be of a slightly different generation, the Eisenhower generation, which had missed the full impact of the experience of World War II. She wanted more innocence to drive Hannah's curiosity about herself and the world than she, Settle, could legitimately muster. Hannah could write the books without really knowing as much as Settle did. Moreover, with Hannah younger, she could actively participate in the young people's revolution in the 1960s and not be, as Settle had been, an enthusiastic witness, a supporter, to be sure, but more witness than actor. And, above all, as the writer of the four previous books of the series, she could be conscious, even acutely self-conscious, about her literary as well as her personal intentions. She could simply and directly make connections between the actions and discoveries of *The Killing Ground* and the other books. And yet there would be some things—as, indeed, there prove to be—that Hannah could not know, but which Settle and perhaps an acutely engaged reader could not help knowing. Hannah is aware of that imaginary reader, too: "The unknown giant, and Johnny Church, shot at Burford, my namesake Hannah, and lovely dangerous Lily are in lost graves, forgotten, except by me and a lone reader who has not been able to sleep either, who is bringing them to life from the books of my search. It has taken us both a long time to give them back their lives" (8).

The split between Settle and Hannah, and with it the establishment of Settle's clear-cut omniscience, is resolved easily enough by having this story told in the same multiple points of view that have come to be characteristic of the entire series—sometimes in third person, both limited and omniscient, and here, especially, often in first person; usually in Hannah's voice and view, though often others tell lengthy first-person stories as well. The story is put together so that Hannah can act and react as a character and, at one and the same time, legitimately comment on the action and on herself, in terms of the whole quintet. Here, for example, she is quite precisely defining herself and her times in section 2 of the book, "Before the Revolution: 1960":

I wonder if anyone in 1960 knew that an era was at an end. We didn't think of it. The whole complacent world was a wall to bounce opinions against while we lived in its glow. We were the Eisenhower children who stamped their feet at Daddy. We had no way to imagine lives free of that benign confinement. But what we did not bother to imagine had already begun. Quietly in the South, nice black boys with crew cuts sat at Woolworth counters in their best sports jackets while we read novels about alienation or power, and went to Martha's Vineyard. We knew people who knew the Kennedys. Our politics that year were sexual. Angry intelligence, talent rising out of poverty, and being Jewish, were tickets to our beds. We had, to them, some evasive scent of power (156).

The Killing Ground is a series of circlings around events, held together with ritual funerals for the dead, told in four separate units: "The Return: June 1978," "Before The Revolution: 1960," "The Beginning: 1960–1980," and an "Epilogue: January 1980." It has an enormous cast of characters; not only are most of the major characters of the first four novels of the quintet remembered and refurbished, but also characters from other fictions of Canona jostle with and against Hannah and the reader. And given time and scrutiny, characters change. For example, Althea Lacey, boy-crazy and insufferable as a girl and later a drunken, desperately cynical wife in *The Scapegoat*, is here revealed as Aunt Althea, a powerful, strong-willed, compassionate old woman of eighty who has done good works. She has much to teach Hannah as, painful layer by layer, Hannah excavates her buried past.

The "Epilogue: January 1980" is Althea's funeral and Hannah's final trip home. She has already come far and learned much. She knows now, for example, why her first version of the story of Johnny McKarkle had not worked, "not knowing yet that forgiveness comes only when the facts are faced, all the way to the font of tears and hope." "It was then that I tried for the first time to set down Johnny's death in words," she (Hannah) continues. "It was too soon. I failed then because I knew too little of the past. The vision was a lie. It lacked distance and empathy. I had not yet seen my father, Mooney, as a tentative boy, or the killing pride of Captain Dan Neill. I had not caught Lily's blind yearning, or seen the child, my mother, in the speckled mirror, become her isolated self" (366–67). She knows that for herself, as for Settle, the change of heart and direction came in the churchyard at Burford. The quest was renewed. It all ends, finally, at the limits of knowledge, at Althea's funeral, where Hannah stands side by side with Jake Catlett, who killed her brother Johnny all those years ago in jail, and is now a "dressed-up well-upholstered hillbilly in his Buick, who I had last seen caged behind bars in the county jail, desperate and skinny." And some of the simple, factual mystery is solved by what Jake tells Hannah:

> She marched right up there, little skinny woman, I never even knew her, and she posted my bond and I walked out between her and Pa, out on bail. I remember standing there in the sun in front of the courthouse and I never knew which way to turn.
>
> All she said was, "This has gone far enough" (374).

It is Aunt Althea, then, whose act of justice and love saved the life of Jake Catlett and now ends the quest of Hannah. Hannah's response to the final, surprising revelations? "Gulfs of things I didn't know shook me. I had been fooled by silence and a past I hadn't shared" (375). And why hadn't Althea in all those years told Hannah? Jake Catlett, once an accidental murderer,

THE BEULAH QUINTET

now a good and decent man, a *changed* man, thanks to the lovingkindness of Aunt Althea, has the answer for that, too:

"Hannar, you can't never see but from where you stand. She wasn't about to tell you nothing."
"Why?"
"She didn't want to."
That was all the explanation I had. All the digging, all the questioning, all the past I'd harrowed ended in that valley where it had begun (376).

And this novel, full of sorrow and surprises, ends with tears for the dead at a graveside and with a vision of the new, the next generation of these families, there in the cemetery where so many of the honored dead, Catletts, Neills, and Laceys, lie buried beneath inappropriately pompous epitaphs:

I was watching a new breed of child, maybe as mistaken as we had been, but at least unafraid of the fathers. Beyond the long knives of the sixties revolution, these children of the next decade had been granted adulthood as a right. It is the only lasting result of revolution I know, when a dream of one generation becomes a right of the next (382).

It needs to be said that in this rich book, with its "stratum on stratum of connection," the wisdom and peace of the brief epilogue is earned. Not only earned, but essential. The length and depth of the quintet demand it. And, intricately, it comes down to something that urgently simple. "Deep within us there had been instilled an itch," Hannah/Settle says at the end, "a discontent, an unfulfilled promise, perpetually demanding that it be kept. Johnny and Thankful, and all of us, would always fail and always win, and eternal vigilance and our sense of loss, of being unblessed, were the price of freedom" (384).

Perhaps in a tribute to Settle's newly established position among our best serious novelists, *The Killing Ground* received mixed notices. Jonathan Yardley was negative, saying that the novel lacked "life and heart."[28] Aaron Latham produced an essentially smart-aleck review for the *New York Times Book Review*, hurting the book's chances in the popular marketplace. "Though she sometimes pollutes her fiction with waste words and waste characters and waste subplots," he wrote, "just when it appears time to close the mine she strikes a rich vein and makes the work of digging through so many words seem worthwhile."[29] Mixed but strongly positive was the notice of Bruce Allen for the *Christian Science Monitor*: "*The Killing Ground* is weakened by Hannah's/Settle's uncompromisingly sardonic mockery of her people's values. At its best, though, this darkly powerful saga, reminiscent of some of Faulkner's best work, compells as by virtue alone of its keen understanding of the ironical shaping power of history."[30]

The place of the whole extraordinary quintet, and the place of *The Killing Ground* within it, remain to be fully known and understood. Time will tell. Meantime the five volumes illustrating and exemplifying our his-

THE BEULAH QUINTET

tory stand as a remarkable achievement, already recognized by some as a major contribution to the literature of the time.

William F. Ryan has a strong reasonable basis for the claim he makes for her work: "Mary Lee Settle may well be remembered as the 20th-century American novelist who most splendidly recorded the passion and ideals of our history."[31]

Notes

1. Granville Hicks, foreword, *O Beulah Land* (New York: Ballantine, 1965) xv.

2. Settle, "Mary Lee Settle," *Contemporary Authors Autobiography Series*, ed. Dedria Bryfonski (Detroit: Gale Research, 1984) 1:322.

3. Roger Shattuck, introduction appearing in all five Ballantine paperback volumes of the Beulah quintet. Here quoted from the first paperback edition of *The Scapegoat* (1982) vii.

4. William J. Schafer, "Mary Lee Settle's Beulah Quintet: History Darkly, Through a Single-Lens Reflex," *Appalachian Journal* 10, 1 (1982): 77–86.

5. Settle, "Recapturing the Past in Fiction," *New York Times Book Review* 12 Feb. 1984: 1, 36–37.

6. C. A. Taormina, "On Time with Mary Lee Settle," *Blue Ridge Review* 1 (1978): 10.

7. Settle, "Mary Lee Settle," 319.

8. Settle, "Mary Lee Settle," 320.

9. Settle, "Recapturing the Past" 36.

10. All direct quotations in the following section, unless otherwise identified, are taken from tape-recorded conversations between Settle and George Garrett in the fall of 1986.

11. Settle, "Recapturing the Past" 36.

12. Settle in conversation. See also "Recapturing the Past" 36.

13. Settle, "Recapturing the Past" 36.

14. Settle, *Prisons* (New York: Putnam, 1973) 38. Further references noted parenthetically are to this edition.

15. Rosemary M. Canfield, *Masterplots II*, 156–57. Canfield's little essay is especially fine on Settle's use of values, positive and negative, in the quintet.

16. Settle, *O Beulah Land* (New York: Viking, 1956) 6. Further references noted parenthetically are to this edition.

17. Settle, *Know Nothing* (New York: Viking, 1960) 9. Further references noted parenthetically are to this edition.

18. William Peden, "Back to Beulah Land," *Saturday Review* 5 Nov. 1960: 33.

19. See Nancy Carol Joyner, "Mary Lee Settle's Connections: Class and Clothes in the Beulah Quintet," *Women Writers of the Contemporary South*, ed. Peggy Whitman Prenshaw (Jackson: University Press of Mississippi, 1984) 165–78.

20. Settle, *The Scapegoat* (New York: Random House, 1980) 146. Further references noted parenthetically are to this edition.

21. Taormina 14.

22. Robert Houston, "Blood Sacrifice," *The Nation* 8 Nov. 1980: 470.

23. Anne Tyler, "Mining a Rich Vein," *The Washington Post Book World* 28 Sept. 1980: 13.

24. E. L. Doctorow, "Mother Jones Had Some Advice," *New York Times Book Review* 26 Oct. 1980: 1, 40–42.

25. Jonathan Yardley, "Scintillating Scapegoat," *The Washington Star* 16 Nov. 1980: F6.

26. Shattuck, introduction, *The Scapegoat*, xiii–xiv.

27. Settle, *The Killing Ground* (New York: Farrar, Straus, 1982) 153. Further references noted parenthetically are to this edition.

28. Jonathan Yardley, "Mary Lee Settle Concludes the Beulah Quintet," *The Washington Post Book World* 13 June 1982: 3.

29. Aaron Latham, "The End of the Beulah Quintet," *New York Times Book Review* 11 July 1982: 1.

THE BEULAH QUINTET

30. Bruce Allen, "Perfect End for a Worthy Series," *Christian Science Monitor* 13 Mar. 1982: B3.

31. William F. Ryan, "Mary Lee Settle and Johnny Rebel," *Virginia Country* May/June 1984: 56.

CHAPTER THREE

Other Novels from Beulah Land

There are three novels which, while not part of the Beulah quintet, are set in the same world and involve some of the same characters. Two, *The Love Eaters* (1954) and *The Kiss of Kin* (1955), are her first novels—*The Kiss of Kin* having, in fact, been written first. The third, *The Clam Shell* (1971), was written after she had, as she believed then, finished the Beulah trilogy. *The Love Eaters* and *The Kiss of Kin* are both set in the fictional city of Canona in a time scheme roughly contemporary with their writing and publication. *The Clam Shell* begins in Canona at a very precise time, the Sunday afternoon of 4 December, 1966 while a group of men and women are gathered together watching on television the football game between the New York Giants and the Cleveland Browns: "All over the eastern part of America there are people who look like us, nice people, either watching the football game or playing bridge." The story begins there, then drops back nearly thirty years to the time these middle-aged people were

OTHER NOVELS FROM BEULAH LAND

of college age and World War II had not yet happened to change everything forever. There are, then, all kinds of relationships between these books—especially *The Clam Shell*, which has many of the same characters as those who populate *The Killing Ground*—and the Beulah quintet: place; a shared past, whether they know much of that past or not; and, not least, a complex relationship to the life of Settle herself, a subtle bending of fact and fiction of the kind that also characterizes at least the last two volumes of the quintet. Certainly these books can add to the reader's understanding and appreciation of the quintet; yet in her design they are peripheral to it, not sharing the central quest nor the overriding classical parallel to that quest, the story of Antigone. Not completely separate then, and indeed quite closely related in the case of *The Clam Shell*, these books must stand alone.

All three had been out of print for a long time until recently. In 1986 Scribner's brought out *The Love Eaters* and *The Kiss of Kin* in their Signature Editions trade paperback line. In 1987 *The Clam Shell* appeared in the same series. Only *The Clam Shell*, for reasons given later, has been revised for this resurrection, a fact which tells us that unlike a good many authors Settle, having arrived at full artistic mastery of her chosen form and, coincidentally, at the peak of public recognition, will still stand by her earliest published work. Of course, she had been writing, seriously dedicated, betting her life on it, for some years before *The Love Eaters* was published. She was not in any sense a beginner. And though it is true that Settle has grown and developed, learned as an artist, as she has written her books, the surprising thing is how fully formed as a writer, demonstrably skilled and in full control of her means and material, she was from the first. Following the publication of *The Love Eaters* she had received excellent, indeed laudatory reviews. In her autobiographical essay she remembers a Sunday morning in Paris at the time of its publication, when she was leaving Paris to return to London. At the last minute, just as the train was beginning to pull out of the Gare St. Lazaire, her friend, the American writer Max Steele (one of the original founders of *The Paris Review*), came running down the platform to present her with some farewell gifts, including newspapers:

> He had found the *Observer* and the *Times*, the two leading London Sunday papers. Alone in the carriage I opened them. Both papers had published glowing reviews of my book. More followed in the next week. It was the most complete acceptance of a "first novel" that anyone could dream of. I had the satisfaction of holding in my hands several cables from American editors, from publishing houses that had refused my book at reader level.[1]

And perhaps equally important as any published reviews, though of course the result of them, was her immediate acceptance as a member in good standing of that closed, hierarchical literary world, the English literary establishment. Had she chosen to continue to write in what she now calls her "acerbic" manner about modern people and problems in recognizable contemporary settings, there would, it seemed, have been a

OTHER NOVELS FROM BEULAH LAND

safe and secure place, if not an especially distinguished one, for her in the literary scene. It needs to be remembered how many of the most highly regarded writers of this century have settled for that much, or less, and with much less risk and with more and easier "success." Two things, among others, freed her from that possibility. In her autobiographical essay she describes her second husband, the Englishman Douglas Newton, as "a fine young poet who had one of the most exciting and incisive minds I have ever been allowed to share." But her success as novelist led to "a new sense of competitiveness that was too much for our companionship to bear." Much happened to her in the years that followed, including personal injury and disillusion; but above and beyond the personal was her beginning of and total commitment to the series of novels which would finally become the Beulah quintet. Once the first volume, *O Beulah Land*, appeared in 1956, her literary situation was distinctly different.

What she had done before, what had earned her success, was recognizable and at least somewhat trendy, if not fashionable. When *O Beulah Land* appeared, the genre of the historical novel was in bad repute; as a result, she has said in interviews and conversations, the critics who had admired her first two books turned their backs on her. She was in effect alone and starting over at the beginning. At least so it must have seemed, "objectively," from the outside. In point of fact she was not following that other pattern, one adhered to by many other writers, usually "unsuccess-

UNDERSTANDING MARY LEE SETTLE

ful" in the earlier work, of turning against her beginnings. As the whole pattern of the Beulah quintet
proves, she was moving toward more and more mastery, toward more freedom and flexibility of form, with
each novel in the series; but she was building on her
experience and knowledge and, more than those, on the
place and people she had claimed as her own in the first
two novels.

When *The Love Eaters* was published, to considerable acclaim, *The Kiss of Kin* had already been written
and had been rejected by most of the publishers in
England and the United States. After the initial challenge to James Broughton ("All right, I'll prove it to you.
I will write the Phaedra as a modern novel"), she began
The Love Eaters. "This seems an awfully intellectual
beginning," she says now, "but that's actually how it
began." She wrote it at Sloane Court West, in an almost
empty room, pulling her bed, "a little cot," up to a table
to write. Many of her future habits and rituals of
creation were already in place or being discovered at
that time. "I was already writing in long sheets in
longhand," she says of the practice she still follows in
her first drafts, even though nowadays she owns and
uses a state-of-the-art word processor and high-speed
printer for letter drafts. "I must have been very fright-
ened of form," she adds, "because in that early book I
literally had a graph on the wall of every chapter and its
name. I knew almost everything in that book before it
began." She does not mention in any detail the habits
and experience she had acquired from writing six full-

length plays. But certainly from the experience of writing for the modern theater she would have, and did, learn to create a clear-cut situation, a strong, forward-moving structure made up of scenic units, and a solid sense of dialogue. Appropriately, she says of *The Love Eaters* that "the image it began with was people arguing over a little theater performance."

The novel is set in Canona, West Virginia, and chiefly concerns the production of a play, *Bedtime for Miranda*, by the Canona Thespians under the direction of a hired professional director from the outside, the Tiresias-like Hamilton Sacks. Its basic situation is described, briefly enough, by Scribner's in jacket copy for the Signature Edition: "A wealthy, small-town theatrical group finds itself at the direction of a chair-bound cripple whose designs extend beyond the stage. And as he begins to lose control, so do his players, revealing appetites they scarcely knew they had." The story opens with the arrival of Sacks and his mother on the C. & O. train (giving Settle a good opportunity to introduce Canona to Sacks at the same time that she does so for the reader) and ends with Sacks and his mother having moved on (for the thirteenth time in fifteen years) after a disaster. The disaster in this case is the destruction by fire of the theater and the death in that fire of the story's beautiful and amoral Hippolytus figure, Selby. The story is almost entirely presentational in the telling—quickly scenic, moving forward by action and dialogue and with minimal description, exposition, and with only the slightest hints of novelistic introspection in any of the large cast of characters. Behind the surface story is the framework of the Phaedra story, myth and plays—in diminished form, of course, as it is played out in alien modern times. As Settle has a number of times remarked, no critic seems to have taken note of the classical parallel here or the classical allusions, the kinds of echoing implication she has continued to use one way and another in all her books.

Other qualities present here that will be found in all her work, in whatever styles and forms, include the capacity of characters to change slightly, or more, each time they reappear. Even in this tight little story the characters are constantly growing and changing as, bit by bit, the reader begins to know them better. They are, as in all her work, often very different from the first impressions of them. And all of them, to one extent or another, misinterpret and misapprehend each other. It follows that the ironies exploited here, subtle or blatant, are often savage. Stylistically, Settle demonstrates a superb ear for speech and for the written language and uses both in interesting juxtapositions. And there is the irrepressible humor, a sense of comedy deeply rooted in her characters' incessant high seriousness about themselves. Here, for example, is the mother of Martha Dodd (the Phaedra figure, central character of the novel) opening a chapter (scene) with a little speech about their background: "We're English blood, all right. Pure English. Your paw always swore his grandmaw was a Jew—but I don't believe it. I seen her plenty times. She was just real dark English—like you. Even sprouted a

OTHER NOVELS FROM BEULAH LAND

little moustache like a man when she got old—you'll get yours. All the side of the family you take after do."[2]

The Kiss of Kin, taken directly from a play of her own, has many of the same quick, lean, minimal characteristics. "I think that the concept, what I thought of at the time," she says in conversation, "was of family relationships breaking down in the face of money and worry. But that's very feeble. . . . What I actually saw was out of my own memory. My mother's family decided every important thing—and it usually had to do with money because it was the Depression—around a large kitchen table at Cedar Grove. And so the image must have been a true memory. Which it very seldom is, by the way."

The Kiss of Kin, also set in West Virginia, takes place in one day, almost exclusively in one place, and involves the gathering of several generations and branches of one family for the funeral and the reading of the will of the family matriarch—Anna Mary Passmore. It is third-person omniscient in point of view, and, like *The Love Eaters*, it advances dramatically, scene by scene, depending in large part on dialogue and presented actions and reactions to make its points and revelations. Although it is a rural book and much more in the tradition and conventions of southern literature, conventions Settle at once uses and changes, it is like *The Love Eaters* in its inexorable accumulation of large and small ironies. And most of the characters receive more justice than mercy from the book's most vital and memorable character, the deceased Anna Mary Passmore, who appears, at the story's denouement in the form and words of a written document, her last will and testament.

Neither of these books reads much like a "first novel." They are highly advanced in mastery of craft; and interestingly, perhaps because they are cut to the bone of speech and action and not burdened with distracting details, neither has become dated much in the thirty-some years since it first appeared. Both books are extremely bright and clever, complete experiences.

It deserves to be noted that the foundation of Settle's critical theory, the theoretical basis of her fiction, was in place by the time she came to write these first two novels. Increasingly, book by book, she would make discoveries of the multiple possibilities of narrative prose, of new and more subtle uses of presentational prose as well as scenes and dialogue. She would see how shifts of point of view on perception could be as dramatic, as much a matter of *showing*, as the spare, objective, unenhanced dramatic scene. The truth is that Settle began, where so many young writers have arrived today, with minimalism, and has moved steadily toward more and more amplitude and resonance. Behind her first books were years of reading and appreciation, the establishment of affiliations with favorite models. Here is how she put that, in reply to a question as to what authors she regularly reads: "Always Conrad, never James Joyce or Henry James (their styles are too easily imitated). Proust always. Dorothy Sayers sometimes. Stendahl usually. These are the ones I reread."[3] And the text for all of it, the text in an almost scriptural, exegetical sense, a text mentioned again and again in interviews, lectures, conversations, and always in her literary or creative writing classes over the years, is Joseph Conrad's preface of 1897 to *The Nigger of the "Narcissus."* From that text there is the celebrated passage, in some ways as mysterious and evocative as any Zen *koan* or mystical mantra, to which Settle returns again and again, that moment when Conrad wrote: "My task which I am trying to achieve is, by the power of the written word to make you hear, to make you feel—it is, before all, to make you *see*! That—and no more, and it is everything! If I succeed, you shall find there according to your deserts: encouragement, consolation, fear, charm—all you demand—and, perhaps, also that glimpse of truth for which you have forgotten to ask."[4]

This ideal with all its implications, which grow and change like any great text, as one grows and changes, has been Settle's model for excellence from the beginning of her career.

The Clam Shell

The Clam Shell, which Settle has called "the closest thing to an autobiographical novel I ever wrote," actually began, she says, as a work of nonfiction, an autobiographical account in the manner of *All the Brave Promises*. Of the beginning of the idea for it Settle has clear and particular memories. In an interview with Garrett she reports:

UNDERSTANDING MARY LEE SETTLE

The conception, the seed planted, of *The Clam Shell*, was planted a long time ago, a long time before I began to write it. And it was during the war, when I left the WAAF and went into the OWI. I was walking through Hyde Park with Archibald MacLeish, who I realize now was in his mid-40s then, maybe mid to late 40s; and as far as he was concerned he was walking through Hyde Park with a pretty young girl and being just a little bit impressive. And I was pleased with that and I liked him. . . . Anyway, he said during that walk: "I've spent the rest of my life finding out that what I knew at eighteen was true." And it stuck in my mind. The concept of *The Clam Shell* was to go back and find out partly if what he said was true, if I did already at eighteen know the seeds of what I knew when I began the book. The other thing that kind of set me off on the book was that, as far as I was concerned, I had written the trilogy and it was finished and it was a failure. And I wasn't going to touch it any more and so on. I wondered where in one's individual life, one's daily span of events, where the heroic archetypes loomed behind it. When you write about heroes, personal life looms unsaid behind the heroes; and I wondered if when you wrote about personal life, about an event that happened, a changing event, if the archetypes, the gods, loomed unwritten behind that. In other words, if it was the opposite. So I went back to my eighteenth year and wrote about the first year that I was at Sweet Briar.

Settle has been fascinated, certainly as early as the writing of *The Love Eaters*, with classical—that is, archetypal—parallels and allusions, with the allusive survival of the deep and ancient myths in modern times, contemporary settings. But this notion was different, at least from a different point of view. Could these same things be not imposed upon or derived from comparison and contrast to present action, but rather called forth, summoned up, by the present action and actors? She had already written in the trilogy how much the past, known and unknown, can impose its patterns, almost its will, upon the present. And she had planted the central, archetypal story, the Antigone story, deeply there. But this was a different sort of question and idea; thinking about it helped to set her free, a little later, to come back and transform the trilogy into the quintet. Thinking on these things inevitably led backwards toward *Prisons* and forward toward, finally, *The Killing Ground*, where Hannah McKarkle is not only conscious of the problem and the questions but also, having written the other four books of the quintet, fully aware of the living influence of Antigone in her present, "one's daily span of events." In that sense, the making of *The Clam Shell*, quite aside from the relative success or failure of it at the time in the fickle marketplace, was seminal for all her work to follow and in that sense a hugely successful undertaking. It helped to free her from the haunting sense of the failure of the trilogy. There is an irony here; for in a purely mundane sense *The Clam Shell* was an even greater failure, the nadir of her career in the United States—a situation she frankly blames on her editor and publisher in America at that time. "It was published here, in America, by Seymour Lawrence/ Delacorte, who had decided that I wasn't going to make him any money [Lawrence/Delacorte had earlier pub-

lished, without notable success, *All the Brave Promises*];
so the book came out literally with magnolias on it, and
totally without advertising. And as far as I know it got
no reviews at all, but I was in Turkey at the time
working on something very exciting and, to me, very
new. I had gone back to the Trilogy which was fast
becoming four books."

The Clam Shell was written in a flat in London, to
which Settle had retreated after the election of President
Nixon, honoring her pledge to leave the country if and
when that happened. "I remember, a couple of weeks
before I left for England," she says, "sitting in an
apartment in the Village watching the New York Giants
football game that I used for the book." She describes
the British publication in much more positive terms,
saying that "it was very carefully and beautifully edited
by James Michie at the Bodley Head." An early draft of
the novel, before Michie exercised any editorial influence on it, is on deposit at the Alderman Library of the
University of Virginia. Even a cursory examination
indicates the validity of Settle's praise for Michie. It
appears to be a model of intelligent, sympathetic editorial excellence.

In a free and easy, elegantly executed first-person,
present-tense narration, chronological after the opening
scene, yet moving adroitly in and out of present time
with past time, past tenses, Settle tells the story, aston-
ishingly accurate in its factual details, of her own
experience of her first year at Sweet Briar, here called
Nelson-Page. Yet though it could conceivably be treated

OTHER NOVELS FROM BEULAH LAND

as strictly autobiographical and in that mimetic mode, part of the *narrator's* autobiography certainly, it also is clearly fiction. It opens with the gathering in 1966, for the Sunday afternoon football game on television, of many of the fictional characters who figured in *The Love Eaters* and will have prominent parts in *The Killing Ground*: Daisy and Maria, Anne Randolph and Plain George Potter, John Boy Crane, the vaguely glamorous and vaguely dangerous Charley Bland (who will kill himself in *The Killing Ground*, set twelve years later). Everybody drinks as the game goes on. It is not a happy scene or a happy time: "The three women want to kill me. They want to splash the white walls with my blood, to fling me between them like a rat in a terrier's teeth."[5] Bad things have happened to these middle-aged people; things have gone bad with their lives:

   None of the women is watching the game. They are
watching the men watch. Anne Randolph touches Plain
George's head and smiles. Since their daughter, Sally B,
killed herself in her car, Plain George and Anne Randolph
have faded closer together than ever in their lives. Maria
watches John Boy. Hatred, which she thinks is concern,
shadows her faded face (12).

What happens in this opening scene, besides the exciting, free-scoring game (Cleveland 49—New York 40), is that the speaker is finally forced out of this circle of friends. Or, at any rate, chooses to step out of "their ever self-healing circle," to face "the American winter which the free must always bear. I wonder if I have the courage to choose that winter, become, to them, a simple comic-book figure in their minds, as heroes and the dead are simple, manageable and always someplace else. Would Ishmael have chosen, or Moses, or all our ancestors? Perhaps, instead of choosing, we force the choice on others'' (21). In the end, to the envy of the others, she goes off with Charley Bland to get drunk.

This is a bold opening, extremely risky, yet extremely important for the effect of the whole book. With the opening of the next chapter the story will have dropped back thirty years in time (same place) to the summer of 1936, just before the girls all went off over the mountains to Nelson-Page in Virginia. For the rest of the story the group, the magic circle, *is* almost magic, thanks to a bright nostalgia, thanks to youth and good looks and good health and high hopes and enough money, if nothing else. All the rest of the story—for the reader will not return again to the sour and sodden time of the opening chapter—is colored brightly by an accurately rendered sense of being young with all the future, like an incredible wealth, left to spend. Much of the rest of the book is comedy, and it ends with a burst of laughter (''We can't stop laughing''); but it will never quite escape the long shadows cast by the opening scene, the awareness of the waste and sorrow which wait patiently for them all, just as, in a different way, the world of 1936 through which they move, with all the youth's urgent and often wholly indiscriminate attention to detail, will be broken to pieces in a few short unimaginable years.

OTHER NOVELS FROM BEULAH LAND

Settle has done a marvelous job with the summoning up of 1936. In a piece she wrote for fellow Sweet Briar alumnae she has recalled some of that year: "It was the year of veils, Hal Kemp, Astaire and Rogers, fitted black Chesterfields, and the word 'sophistication.'"[6] All these things, the things of the moment, are there and used to great advantage. There are knock-knock jokes; there are new products like Dentyne gum; there are wonderful cars, none grander than Charley Bland's La Salle (Plain George has his own black Oldsmobile); there are the movie stars—Katharine Hepburn is starring in *Mary of Scotland*; music comes from Skinnay Innis and Coleman Hawkins, Nellie Lutcher and Dwight Fisk; there is a litany of popular tunes—"Moonglow," "Night and Day," "Sweet Lorraine," "You're the Top," "Stardust," "Temptation," and many more. There are political and social events: the 1936 Nazi Olympics, the affair of Edward and Wally, the Roosevelt versus Landon campaign and election ("Landon, Landon, he's my man./Throw Roosevelt in the garbage can"). The book the narrator carries with her to read on the C. & O. pullman on the trip to Nelson-Page is, of course, *Gone with the Wind*. Here the narrator views herself as seen by her father as he drives her to the station:

Now I am his green dream, his princess, his sweetheart of Sigma Chi, if I'll shut up for fifty yards more across the bridge, not mention *The New Republic* or the war in Spain, or Roosevelt, or Norman Thomas, or the Future Gold Star Mothers, until he gets me across the river and into the Chesapeake and Ohio Fast Flying Virginian going east and delivers me safely to the training ground he wants for his kind, where the red-necked Jews and sex-mad Negros and the lean-thighed mountain boys, the bastard kin inside my own muscles, can't get inside the club gates of my dear dry decent little territory (83).

Following the opening chapter there is another establishing chapter set in Canona, which is necessary as contrast to the insecurity of the new strange world of Nelson-Page. Then a full academic year at Nelson-Page, from arrival, with a homecoming chapter during Christmas vacation when the "sophistication" of the young group in the city is set against the plainness of Christmas dinner with their kin in the country, on through the year, ending with an Elizabethan May Day (or Derby Day; they can hear the band playing "My Old Kentucky Home" on somebody's radio). There is a set piece weekend at the University of Virginia, seen from the point of view of an overwhelmed, slightly drunk, pursued young woman, a sequence that surely challenges, and perhaps bests, the more celebrated one by William Styron in *Lie Down in Darkness*. A young lover, Jack Story, works hard at relieving the narrator of her virginity, but always fails—even in an attempted rape, the result of which is that she gets punished for being late getting back and acquires a reputation for being "wild." She is unjustly tried and punished by her peers in a brisk formal "trial." It was this event that was the basic image for the book, Settle writes in *Contemporary Authors Autobiography Series*: "My concern in the book was to explore a trial in a room at Sweet Briar on a sunny afternoon and see if it shadowed the greater trials, the battles, the demands for freedom I was already writing about as an adult." This scene is comic and so is the punishment, though not without injustice; but behind it, as behind the same women watching the men watch football in 1966, loom the tall, savage archetypes of the Furies.

But, as much as anything else, the novel is about education and the one wonderful teacher, here named Anson Trevor Spaulding, who brings her to poetry, to Wordsworth, then to Eliot, Auden, St. John Perse, even to Stephen Spender. "I take the thin books from Faber and Faber in London out of the library. They litter the floor. I think continually of those who were truly great, and stop going to classes" (183). He mourns the death of Lorca in that year. By example and precept he teaches her irony and pity, contempt and compassion for her enemies, qualities which will set her on her quest, never quite invulnerable but able to choose freedom when the time for choice arrives.

In that sense, though *The Clam Shell* is her most autobiographical book in terms of events which are close to those of her own life, it is quite evidently true that Johnny Church and Lily Lacey, who choose freedom at the highest cost, are her most autobiographical characters. In a short time after the events of *The Clam Shell*, Settle would have very little in common with the young woman of that story. Except in what she had learned. Fiction, she was to learn, by doing it, can become the purest form of autobiography. And, conversely, autobiography, with little more than a gesture, can become fiction.

Speaking of *The Clam Shell* and its curious and close relationship to people and events in her life, in an interview with the author of this study she says:

It really did start out to be a fragment of autobiography. But, of course, what it turned out to be was a novel. As people who can't write fiction because they cannot accomplish the transmutation, almost like alchemy, of the raw material of personal life into fiction, the people who can't do that, make that, write autobiography and call it fiction. I was writing fiction and thinking it was autobiography, because that transmutation is natural to me.

This is what she learned by doing *The Clam Shell*, and from the "raw material" of it she saw how much the stranger who was herself at eighteen had known in advance of the experience which would confirm intuition with hard facts and knocks.

Notes

1. Settle, "Mary Lee Settle," *Contemporary Authors Autobiography Series*, ed. Dedria Bryfonsk: (Detroit: Gale Research, 1984) 1:316.

2. Settle, *The Love Eaters* (New York: Harper, 1954) 137.

3. *Bulletin of Sweet Briar College* Apr. 1979:1.

OTHER NOVELS FROM BEULAH LAND

4. Joseph Conrad, preface to *The Nigger of the "Narcissus"* (Oxford University Press, World's Classics series, 1984) xlii.

5. Settle, *The Clam Shell* (Seymour Lawrence/Delacorte) 10. Further references noted parenthetically are to this edition.

6. Settle, "The Editor's Room," *Sweet Briar College Alumnae Magazine* Fall 1978:34.

CHAPTER FOUR

Blood Tie and *Celebration*

The two novels by Mary Lee Settle in which the setting and focus are primarily foreign, outside of America, *Blood Tie* and *Celebration*, though separated in creation by almost a decade, seem to come, as it were, from opposite ends of her life and career. In 1974, having lived for three years in Bodrum, Turkey, where she had finished *Prisons*, she "had to leave Turkey."[1] Her proximate cause for returning to America, from which she had exiled herself in 1969 following the election of Richard Nixon, was the outbreak of the Cypriot War and the fact that she was almost out of money. But the deeper reason for her return was that she had already begun a novel about Turkey, tentatively titled *The Nth Crusade*.[2] She had begun, as she writes in her piece for *Contemporary Authors Autobiography Series*, but she "could not find the psychic distance in Turkey which is so necessary to writing fiction." Her luck changed slowly at first; a grant from the Merrill Foundation came when she was down to her last two

BLOOD TIE AND *CELEBRATION*

hundred dollars. This allowed her to rent a room, Room 19 of the Colonnade Club on the Lawn of the University of Virginia, where she completed a full draft of the novel.[3] The fall of 1975 and spring of 1976 were spent teaching at Bard and the University of Iowa, and it was at the latter, when she was without a publisher and almost without hope, that editor Theodore Solotaroff, visiting to give a lecture, read the manuscript and recommended it to Houghton Mifflin.

Blood Tie was finally published in 1977 (she was already hard at work on *The Scapegoat*), and in the early spring of 1978 her life "changed completely" when she won the National Book Award for Fiction. There was the brief, disappointing period during which some journalistic critics and reviewers complained that the prize probably should have gone to other, better-known writers. But that turned around, in part as a result of J. D. O'Hara's piece in *The Nation*, which chastized the complaints of other critics and praised the book highly.[4] After *Blood Tie* soon came recognition, awards, honorary degrees, more money and time for her work, and her happy marriage to William Tazewell. It seemed entirely appropriate that an interview for the "Arts and Books" section of *The Washington Star* could be headlined "Life Sings So Sweetly for Settle."[5] And indeed it was a wonderfully productive period for Settle. She finished and brought out *The Scapegoat* and then concluded the Beulah quintet with *The Killing Ground*. Both of these books received the full and prominent attention of the reviewers, and she was even accorded that second

conventional stage of American literary fame—a few
strong attacks on her work, together with the praise of
peers whom she respected.

It was at this point that she wrote her lengthy essay
for the *Contemporary Authors Autobiography Series*, an-
nouncing that she was already "working on *Celebration*,
a novel set in New York State, Kurdistan, Africa and
London." Adding a picture of peace and contentment:
"I live the kind of bourgeois daily life which is so hard
to find, and which is ideal for those whose sustained
task is to put words on paper as honestly as they can.
We paint the house and raise a garden and watch
"M*A*S*H" on television. We cook and entertain our
friends. I long for the simple semiboredom which seems
to drive other women into extremes of anger and
denial."[6] All this biographical detail is mentioned here
not merely because Settle has made literary use of much
of it, in translated form, in the fiction; but also because
one would expect the two books, the one written at a
very low point and the other from a position of security
and confidence, to be fundamentally different. One
would expect *Blood Tie* to be, at the least, darker and
more negative; and one might infer from the title that
Celebration would represent a far more cheerful point of
view. That neither expectation is quite correct or appli-
cable is the result of a number of things worthy of
consideration. First of these may be the fact that the
outline of her life, even in some detail, lacking the fuller
sense of context and connections found in fiction, is raw
material and can never offer up enough significant

BLOOD TIE AND *CELEBRATION*

information to allow for full knowledge or permit much sound judgment. In Settle's fiction one is always given a context for lives and events. And one is then encouraged to weigh and sift and to try to come to judgments, even though the more familiar readers are with her work, the more they know that her characters are often contradictory, paradoxical creatures. Thus the many connections of characters to the real life of Mary Lee Settle are not by any means meaningless, yet they have full meaning only in the imaginary context of her fiction. Behind all of it, clearly, is a person, the author, whose aesthetic, ethical, and spiritual values, though constantly tried and tested and always under interrogation, are too deeply felt and consistently maintained to be much changed by superficial circumstances. Her sense of artistic obligation, of dedication, not so much transcends her life's circumstances (for she is never abstract from the living surfaces of things) as exists somewhat independently. Both books are, in her own terms, strongly affirmative stories. Yet by the same token both books share an unflinching dark vision of the exceedingly dangerous world of these times.

Settle as author can be as contradictory and paradoxical (and mysterious) as any of her own characters. The years that led her to Bodrum were hard ones, and there were hard times there and afterward; yet it is clear there was great joy in those years in her life and in her work. Similarly, the years of contentment between *Blood Tie* and *Celebration* were marred by her battle with cancer, something that was not known beyond her most intelligent common sense. Official lingos of all kinds, like Dr. Dangle's, are accurately evoked and satirized for their inadequacy. Here Teresa's response is on a different, truer, plainer level of speech and reinforces, by contrast, the pompous inadequacy of Dr. Dangle. And contrasting with both is the very precise language, in the first of the two sentences which form this brief paragraph, of the narrator, a language which is not exactly spoken in its syntax but seems more written, though simple and straightforward enough. It is one of the subtle signs by and through which the reader can know, almost intuitively when fully engaged and reading with empathy, when one is dealing with objective narration, at an angle from and outside of a character's vision, and the formulations of a single character. Settle is a master of the art of deftly slipping in and out of the voices of her characters' perceiving, thinking, and remembering, and the voice of the narrator. Here, for instance, in *Blood Tie*, describing the few precious items, the things her grandmother called "pretties," Ariadne had carried with her all across the world, giving a certain sameness to all her rooms in all places, Settle as narrator steps aside from the flow of Ariadne's thinking to offer a corrective comment: "She thought that this designed sameness she carried with her for safety was individual and conscious, not realizing that her habits were as primal as a Bedouin woman's, who sets up her permanencies every night, or that her belongings, her endearments, were of the kind a woman carries slung over her shoulder to run before war or nature."[8] An

BLOOD TIE AND *CELEBRATION*

What was the lipstick doing there? The concept was complex and subtle. "I never wanted to write *Blood Tie*," she says in conversation. "I was pushed into it by circumstances around me, by the sense that you could live any place and find . . . oh, not 'a community of interests' and all that bullshit, but a pulse of living in common. And this was as alien a territory as I had ever been in to find that pulse. Asia Minor is an evocative, explosive, wild, energy-laden, dry, arid part of the world." The kinds of meticulous research she demands of herself were mostly exercised in Virginia. There in the neighborhood of the Cow Pasture River she went in the company of geologists to study caves. And in one of these, a place aptly called Refrigerator Cave, she and others swam across a dark underground lake, carrying candles and matches in a plastic bag, to test the validity of Timur's cave experience in *Blood Tie*.

The actions and events of *Blood Tie* take place chronologically during 1972 in the imaginary Turkish coastal town of Ceramos, closely modeled on Bodrum and evoked, at the beginning at least, as a serenely beautiful and "unspoiled" place, with its ruined crusaders' castle and its sacred mountain, "Mount Latmos, now called Annadağ," the mountain where, as the myths had it, Endymion lay sleeping. There are the town and a nearby ancient village, and over across a mile of glorious Aegean Bay there is the uninhabited island of Yazada. There is a large cast of characters, both foreign and Turkish, who play significant parts in the story. Among the foreigners are Ariadne Schrader, a

UNDERSTANDING MARY LEE SETTLE

Virginian who has lived there since 1969 when (like Mary Lee Settle) she came from the Greek island of Kos, initially described as "another middle-aged, divorced American woman, brave and half-alive" (13). Lisa Stewart, the young, rich daughter of Ariadne's friend Jamie Stewart from Culpeper County, Virginia; Trader and Miranda, retired from Plainfield, New Jersey, and living on a yacht, he a sweet and gentle and simple man, she (unbeknownst to him) an urgently insensitive nymphomaniac; Frank Proctor, the CIA man; Horst, the German archaeologist; David, the Dutch Jew who runs a bar in Ceramos; Basil, a sad and bitchy British homosexual. The important Turkish characters include Munci, seaman and sponge fisherman and superb skindiver; Timur, a young man from the nearby village who has fought his way into a university where he has become a radical; his mute younger brother, Kemal; Meral, the mother of these two; Dürüst Osman, an old man, a fighter from the days of Atatürk who now owns most of Ceramos, among other things; Huseyin, the young mayor; Turgut Bey, Istanbul businessman; Vahshi Güven, an ancient smuggler; Kachakchı Attila, the donkey driver; the Chief of Police, the Captain of the Gendarmes, and the new young judge; Melek, the mother of Munci. These are all characters of some importance to the plot or the texture of the story, or both. There are many others who have their brief moments in the light; for instance a chorus of Ceramian women—Gül, Fatma, Hatije; Dervish Mustafa and Crazy Mehmet, sailors; Ohran, the father of Kemal and

BLOOD TIE **AND** *CELEBRATION*

Timur; Hassan, the tailor; Demir, the police spy; Zephyr, the maid of Dürüst Osman; Giglio, the Italian; not to ignore the imaginary Hizir, "the stranger who always came to help in time of trouble." And in a brief, cut-away contrasting section, set in Virginia and Washington, D.C., there are Jamie Stewart; Lewis, his black servant; Bob MacKay, his lawyer, and MacKay's secretary-mistress, Sport. There is Lefty Leftwitch of the State Department; and in a memory sequence Ariadne's former husband, Roger, is indelibly (if briefly) drawn. These characters are of all ages and backgrounds. The Turks are as distinctly different from each other as the foreigners. Some—the Chief of Police, the young judge, the Captain of the Gendarmes—are in effect exiles, sent there from very different parts of Turkey. Others are exiles from the Greek islands. Munci, for example, though his roots are deep in Ceramos, thinks of himself in terms of his immemorial background, as a Cretan.

To go beyond the extraordinary listing of the primary members of the cast, one must add the observation that somehow, in a book of relatively moderate length (386 pages) and with quite enough plot, physical action, and dramatic events to satisfy the demands and definition of a thriller, the reader nevertheless gets to know all of these characters and some of them, a surprising number, very well. And, in a manner that is at once inherent and essential to this story, each character is allowed to develop and demonstrate an entirely individual point of view.

The way this is managed, the way it *happens to* the

reader, is a fascinating joining together of narrative technique with theme. The story proceeds swiftly and chronologically (allowing, however, for flashbacks and memories and recollections) by means of a series of very rapid shifts of point of view. Essentially the overall point of view of the novel is clearly third-person omniscient, but it offers variations on that strategy. Omniscience is, of course, predicated and required for the narrator, taking the reader hand in hand, not only to be able to offer objective scenic and narrative sequences, but also to slip in and out of the limited and specific consciousness of a couple of dozen major and minor characters. It is a close parallel to techniques of cinematic narrative, though often presenting and dramatizing details of interior life in ways that cinematic art has only found the means to hint at.[9] The alternation, then, is between a cameralike omniscient narrator and the limited third-person view of a given character. This method is strongly established at the outset when the reader is plunged directly into the festive, and ritual, occasion of the sacrifice of a ram to mark the launching of a ship in the harbor. The narrator presents details objectively:

The rigging of the boats in dry dock hummed in the new wind. The men took their places at the oak cradle that held the ship poised above the wooden slipway green with sea algae, waiting to carry her into the water. The chant began, chant and thud of heavy mallets against the log struts. The hull began to move; the chanting quickened, the logs tipped toward the sea. Released, the hull slid fast into the harbor, lifting a wave of spume with her stern. The men aboard ran to the ropes, corralling her as she felt the new freedom of the water under her, plunged, and threatened to turn. As they tamed her, she rode the harbor calmly, smaller than she had been on land. One by one the bloody hand prints disappeared in the water (5).

A timeless scene. It might be now or centuries ago. It is almost purely "objective," in the sense that it is almost wholly presentational and without judgment; though the paragraph does, like the book of which it is a part, move inexorably from precise detail toward metaphor, taking the ancient grammatical metaphor of a ship as female and using that as if the ship were alive.

The story swiftly moves into the flow of the lives and viewpoints of the crowd of characters who are known at first only as names and presences. Appropriately this is very much a book of the body; all the characters are intensely conscious of their own bodies and the bodies of others. Exposition is minimal at this stage, for expository matters and details are developed throughout the narrative. Some facts of the kind conventionally presented early are not known until late in the story. For example, Ariadne's full name is not learned and used until it becomes a factor in the story itself, on page 246. Similarly David's true name (Hayim) and the story of his desperate childhood during World War II in Holland is not revealed until (pp. 314–20) a group of characters, sailing together on a five-day yachting trip, tell stories about themselves. Just so, it is in the final sequence of the novel, the celebration of the fiftieth

UNDERSTANDING MARY LEE SETTLE

anniversary of the modern Turkish nation, when it is revealed that the ruthless old landlord, Dürüst Osman, was a revolutionary, too, in his time, one of Atatürk's soldiers: "It was the one time of the year when the old man unbent and joined a celebration. He was the last man left alive in the town who had been a soldier of the Gazi. He wore his black kalpak, the gray blanket coat, the black boots of the army of the Gazi. Crisscrossed across his breast were cartridge belts. He wore a dagger that flashed when he turned to speak to Turgut Bey, who looked hot and fretful" (379).

The characters are known first as appearances, then as types, finally and gradually as complex human beings. Thus one begins to know the people of the book much as one might get to know people in life. First impressions are formed often based on handy stereotypes and convenient labels, which impressions are subsequently reinforced, modified, or significantly changed as more and more is learned about the characters. Thus, adding to the basic suspense elements of the plot—will Ceramos be soon ruined by planned development? will Timur, the radical hiding in a cave in Mount Latmos, be caught by the brutal Captain of the Gendarmes? will Huseyin do right or wrong by Lisa? etc.— is the strong element of suspense concerning each of the characters. Simultaneous with separate actions and the working out of events, there are gradual series of revelations concerning each of the characters; the principals being returned to most frequently, which increase knowledge of them more and more until, as important

BLOOD TIE AND *CELEBRATION*

things happen to them, the reader also is able to *feel* the impact of events, of their joys and sorrows, more and more. The key to this empathy, what can make it work, hand in glove with story, is that though there may be *consistency* of character, there can never be simple repetition. No redundancy. Any redundancy would slow the forward drive of the story too much and would have a negative effect on the realization of characters, implying that the reader already knows all there is to know about them. So each adventure into the point of view of an individual character must add to and slightly change our view of that character. The characters must simultaneously satisfy formed expectations and yet manage to surprise. All of this must be accomplished within the context of an accessible narrative with a life and force of its own, and must be done concisely. It requires an elegant arranging and fine-tuning on the part of the author. And it demands a good deal from the reader, as well, not least the concentration of close attention and the capacity to be drawn in, imaginatively engaged in the story, while much of it seems at the beginning as full of questions, as puzzling as an experience in "real life."

Fully to appreciate and enjoy the novel the reader must bring to it as much of life experience as aesthetic or literary experience. All of which sounds much more complicated and difficult for the reader than it is. As in the case of any worthwhile fiction, one must learn to let go, to surrender at least some reticence and join energies with those of the story, to appreciate it fully, to *understand* it. One is prepared for this experience when dealing with works by well-known and established modern (or, for that matter, postmodern) masters. The masters often have a standing reputation for "difficulty," which is in itself a challenge; and other writers conventionally announce their complexity by artificial devices which call attention to themselves. But we are less prepared to deal with a fiction that is characterized by its clarity and accessibility, by dealing with matters of some general interest, and yet equally informed by strong demands for attention and empathy. The irony here is that readers have had much less trouble with *Blood Tie* than professional reviewers. Perhaps the latter, pressured by time and deadlines and the mountains of books waiting for their attention, simply do not have time or inclination to commit themselves to the experience of reading for pleasure.

One point indelibly made in the working out of the story is that no character, Turkish or European or American, fully understands any other character. It begins even on the level of names: Basil sounds to the Turks like their word for *germ*; Frank is their version of a word for *foreigner*; Munci, meanwhile, is called Monkey, though not to his face, etc. More than simply misunderstanding each other they repeatedly misapprehend and misjudge each other—and themselves. Only the reader is in a position to see how these characters, even the best of them (and there are a good many admirable people in *Blood Tie* as well as a number who seem beyond all repair or redemption) deceive and misunderstand and torment and/or flatter themselves.

BLOOD TIE AND *CELEBRATION*

Settle has added an important dimension to the modern fiction of exile and the clash of cultures. On a primary level the cultures of Turkey and the West are distinctly different, and are so presented in the novel; the differences lead to some serious misunderstandings, about matters large and small, and to confrontations and clashes of one kind or another. People are hurt because of cultural differences. And yet the Turkish characters are shown, with interest but without a wink of sentimentality, to be as much the victims of their own misapprehensions, about themselves and each other, as the Europeans and Americans. Clichés—the dangerous innocence of the Americans, the ancient cynicism and corruption of the Near East—are exploited, examined, put to the test, and prove to be inadequate even as one comes to understand how they came to be. Misunderstanding, of self and others, proves to be tragic in *Blood Tie* and proves to be an almost ineradicable characteristic of the human condition. (It is not by accident that Ariadne has Martin Buber's *I and Thou* among her precious books; not irrelevant, either, that it is dusty, long overlooked.) The lives of these people, and several deaths, are played out against the background of history (the ever present crusaders' castle, the village fountain with its carved memories of ancient Greece, the sea bottom with its riches of shards and amphorae) and of the ancient myths—Endymion's mountain where Timur uncovers a real, historical treasure trove confirming myth. The tragedy for many of the central characters, and the best of them, is sadly serious, as is the fate of

BLOOD TIE AND *CELEBRATION*

the boat carrying Ariadne away forever has departed. He has left a handkerchief dipped in the blood of his brother, Timur, together with some of Timur's books, in the secret treasure cave. With dirt and stones he has closed the chamber so that no one else can find it. He has sat still watching the evening sky from the sacred cave and been possessed by a vision of the cosmos:

> The bowl of the sea and the bowl of the sky and us be-tween it he had said sitting here in the evening. It was called, he said, a sphere. Timur said it wasn't real. He was usually right but that time he was wrong. It was real. It was the whole world and people disappeared out of it like Ariadne Hanım on the boat. Timur disappeared out of it, the sphere that he could see (385).

Coming home, down the mountain toward his village, the boy begins to cry, in spite of himself. And his throat hurts. He hears a howl:

> He could feel his mouth stretching wide, somebody pull-ing it, a voice in it too big for it. It hurt.
> "HELE HELE!" the voice howled out to the valley. It was his own, his own voice. He could hear it echo on the rocks. He sounded like a frog.
> He began to run down the mountain to tell his mother (386).

Another affirmative point is simple enough. If the reader, guided by the direction of the narrator, can finally understand the characters and come to some conclusions about them, then it is proved, by demonstration, that such understanding is at least *possible*; proved that alienation (no matter how fashionable a condition of much contemporary fiction) is neither absolute nor inevitable. Readers are not given any godlike, complete omniscience, but are allowed a slightly different angle of vision, a different light upon events that can at least allow them to realize and to assert that the tragic consequences of *Blood Tie* need not have happened. There were places, as in all tragedy, where another turn, another choice, another piece of information missed or misunderstood, might have made all the difference.

On a more conventional critical level a good deal could be said about *Blood Tie* and how it relates to the twentieth-century tradition of the literature of cultural clash and confrontation, starting with Conrad if not much earlier and progressing on through such modern classics as *A Passage to India* or the novels of V. S. Naipaul, masterworks like *A Free State* or *A Bend in the River*. Mentioning Naipaul likewise summons up the subjects of exile and expatriation, certainly a strong current in our literature since the First World War. Here it need only be said that *Blood Tie* and *Celebration* stand in the company of the finest of their kind. Though powerfully and sensitively American books, they belong to world literature.

Another subject worthy of examination in Settle's work, and especially in *Blood Tie*, where the shards of the gods and of ancient cultures are part of present

BLOOD TIE AND *CELEBRATION*

action, is the allusive use of classical myth. Ariadne, of course, is conscious of some of the implications of her own name: Ariadne, daughter of King Minos of Crete and sister of Phaedra; Ariadne who furnished the sword and the thread by which Theseus killed the Minotaur and escaped from the labyrinth; Ariadne who was then abandoned by Theseus on the island of Naxos. More than once Ariadne thinks of herself as abandoned on Naxos. Over the whole story, as the mysterious mountain rises over the city, is the myth of Endymion, a myth which, thanks to many artistic and literary associations, and especially the Keats poem "Endymion," has come to stand for the beauty of youth, for the dream of youth everlasting. In the most familiar version of the story Endymion, a shepherd, lay naked and asleep on Mount Latmos and was seen and desired by the goddess of the moon. She made love to him in his dreams and now he remains there, immortal, forever young and beautiful, and asleep for all time. Youth and beauty, particularly male beauty (and the kinds of desire of women for that male youth and beauty), figure strongly in the story. And the sense of loss. And the hint of a kind of immortality, as in the case of Timur, whose beautiful body is ruined and desecrated when he is killed by the Captain of the Gendarmes, but whose spirit lives on in the memory of others and in the secret chamber of the mountain. Thus that classical myth, taken together with other kinds of allusions to myth and history, functions—never mechanically, but always by teasing implications—to give resonance to the story. It is as if the

BLOOD TIE AND *CELEBRATION*

have created more serious friction among the characters than in *Blood Tie*. And there are some problems of what novelist Doris Betts, in an essay review of the novel, has called "mistranslations of reality."[10] Yet there are far fewer misunderstandings among the central characters; for this story, as it develops, is much less concerned with the swarm of misapprehensions which separate tribe from tribe and one from the other than it is with the possibilities of shared experience, shared life on this planet, the commonality (the *commonwealth* in the old-fashioned sense of the word) of humanity which can transcend intricate differences and details. Life is precious to all these people, each a veteran who has come close to death.

The character who stands squarely at the center of the story is Teresa Cerrutti, a young and recently widowed anthropologist who is recovering from a cancer operation and who has come to London from a teaching job in New York, in part to escape a season of mindless harassment and what she feels, in a larger sense, is the dangerously oppressive political and social climate of the United States in the first term of President Nixon. At the beginning her story is linked to the special concerns of *Blood Tie*. She and her new husband, Michael, an archaeologist, go into a remote area of eastern Turkey, Malakastan, where the Derebey, or local tribal leader, is British educated and interested in many of the same things. "Is it not most interesting, really almost a miracle," he says, "that we have in this one small valley a living museum of customs and

BLOOD TIE AND *CELEBRATION*

hood friend of hers and an aristocratic homosexual (perhaps the most sympathetically and intelligently drawn homosexual drawn by a heterosexual author in our contemporary literature) and brings him together with her friends and her acquaintances at Battestin Crescent. These include: Beverly Evans-Thomas, a former colonial civil servant and the landlord; a quarrelsome English couple, Robin and Penelope Stroud; Artemesia Ambler, the editor of *Fuck* magazine; a beautiful ("Abdul Salim was so beautiful that it was hard to look at him for fear of being caught staring" [122]) Moslem doctor. The group will soon include the also beautiful Yezidi girl ("a beautiful, delicate girl with the eyes of a small boy who hasn't been caught yet." [38]) Zephyr, daughter of the enormously wealthy leader of all the tribe in that part of Turkey where Teresa and Michael had gone. And there are other lesser but memorable characters: Paddy and Knobby, a couple of Irishmen who live at the Jesuit Ogilvie House, with Father O'Malley and Father Pius Deng, and who steal (and ultimately return) a Cezanne as a political act; Jesus Ngoro, an African far from home, dying in Wormwood Scrubbs Prison, whom Pius Deng gracefully sees out of this world. And a good many others, not to ignore the imaginary African (a kind of opposite to Munci's Hizir in *Blood Tie*) Abou Baba Moosa, whom Pius names as a mysterious force for disorders, large and small.

What happens here, together with the love story of the wounded pair, Teresa and Ewen, and an accounting of events in the days of London in 1969, is that they all tell their stories, stories that are listened to and serve to change the listeners. In the beginning the Derebey sets the tone and style for the whole book:

> The Derebey began in English. "As it says in *Alice*, as you no doubt remember, 'Begin at the beginning and go on until you come to the end: then stop.' That is good literary advice. But now I will tell a story within a story within a story within a story that does not come to the end, for that is more like life." He put on his storytelling voice, and I could feel patience all around me in the twilight (39).

As in *The Canterbury Tales*, there are stories within stories, lives within lives. Noel tells of his life in Hong Kong and his tragic love affair with the Chinese boy, Wei Li, in the days before and during the cultural revolution in China and the riots in Hong Kong. Ewen tells (finally unburdening himself in confession before he can marry Teresa) of the African trip where he first fell in with his kinsman Gordie, from Scotland, and some other brutal mercenaries and where he was at least an accessory to murder; and where he was saved, both from execution and malaria, by Father Deng—Pius— who had learned to read English from Conrad's *Heart of Darkness* and *The Shadow Line*. Pius becomes in the flesh the living version of an old mental companion, aptly described by Doris Betts as "an intangible 'black monk' who lives in the mind of Teresa Cerrutti—a figure composed of psychic fragments from her own Jungian animus, Chekhov's story, a remembered childhood friend, a foreshadowing of the real Pius, and what we

BLOOD TIE AND *CELEBRATION*

might call her own soul-voice or conscience."[11] Betts's brief account of the "real Pius," in the same review, is excellent: "At the heart of Mary Lee Settle's ninth novel," she writes, "is a Jesuit priest named Pius, 6' 9", originally a prince in his native Dinka tribe, a nigger in the city surrounding Georgetown University where he studied, a nignog in the book's setting of London, but 'priest everywhere. He clung to that, as he clung to that old rugged cross till its burden at last he could lay down. That had been the first song he had learned in Washington, D.C. the first time he had been invited anywhere'." For the young Teresa and Ewen, being given a second chance at life, and a life together, Noel becomes the pedagogue of the wisdom of the world, the understanding of experience. Here he tells Teresa what she has in common with her lover, Ewen, and so, implicitly, with them all:

"You've started speaking the same language. Yes. The Styx. . . . It's whatever you've faced you can't retreat from. It's a stillness. Veterans have it, and old, surviving whores. After it, you're more alive, not less. You see more clearly, or you can't bear your own awareness and you take to drugs or vice or kill yourself some other way; all of that is so boring and cowardly, I think. With drugs or vice you just end up with your looks gone and your bowels in a mess. How did you get to the well? How did Ewen?" (171).

It is given to Pius to present the inward and spiritual sense of the novel in the form of a wedding present, a pre–World War I globe which he had found in the Portobello Road market:

"You see, like this globe, this room contains a world, a globe you can't see. It was in this room that we stepped on the moon and saw ourselves blue in space, a little pendant orb, and here tonight we celebrate a wedding of each other, a wedding of the soulscapes that in this room make up that world. . . . Here you see Ewen going down the Great Rift to Africa, across the Serengeti, and here am I in the jungle and we are both going across Sudan and down the Nile to Khartoum and then to Cairo, and then we come to Victoria Air Terminal. A miracle!"

He whirled the globe again, playing with it and with her. "Here comes Teresa from New York State in America, and here am I in Washington, and here"—he whirled the globe again—"is Noel come all the way from Hong Kong in the inscape of his soul. . . . Here comes Mr. Evans-Thomas from Malaya, and Mr. Abdul from India, and here we are back again, the whole mind globe, here in this room, as Mr. Eliot, the poet said, Now and in England. So I have given you the world and where we have all been and can go again any time we are silent" (347).

After the celebration in honor of the wedding of Teresa and Ewen, a gathering which brings everyone together again—even Frank Proctor (who has just been reassigned to Turkey)—for the first time since the moon landing; after the happy celebration the book comes suddenly and swiftly to a close. Pius, walking home, pauses to pray for the wedding ("after that he saw and heard nothing but the prayers, and felt nothing but the prayer beads moving through his hands [351]") and is jumped and killed in the dark by some savage London youths. The final scene is the funeral Mass for Pius at the Farm Street Church of the Jesuits, and then "standing beside the path through the gray snow at the Jesuit plot at St. Mary's, Kensal Green." Because the death of Pius and the funeral of Pius came so quickly and briefly, the longer wedding sequence and celebration overwhelms them (as was intended), so that any number of reviewers, including Doris Betts, slightly misremembered, remembered out of sequence: "*Celebration*, which ends with two ceremonies, a funeral and a wedding, leaves no uncertainty about Settle's recognition of death and her celebration of life. Even the book's cover [jacket] shows the mythical snake and Michael's death snake juxtaposed against the mythical flower-mandala of fruition and life."[12]

Certainly *Celebration* represents the fruition of Settle's art so far, her richest, most daring and ambitious work and, taken together with the powerful *Blood Tie*, represents the most successful and serious *international* fiction written by an American in our time.

Notes

1. Settle, "Mary Lee Settle," *Contemporary Authors Autobiography Series*, ed. Dedria Bryfonski (Detroit: Gale Research, 1984) 1: 320.

2. Joe Heumann, "An Interview with Mary Lee Settle," *The Daily Iowan* (Iowa City) 16 Apr. 1976: 10B.

CHAPTER FIVE

Other Works

All the Brave Promises

If, as Settle has said, *The Clam Shell* is her only overtly autobiographical work of fiction, then *All the Brave Promises* (1966) is, thus far, her single fully autobiographical book, a nonfiction personal memoir, created in the 1960s, dealing with her life, beginning in 1942 when she left America to serve in Britain in the Women's Auxiliary of the Royal Air Force. Settle was certainly one of the first, and one of the very few, Americans to serve in the WAAF. She was a volunteer and that, in itself, was highly unusual. As she explains in the opening paragraph of her first chapter:

By January, 1942, all women in Britain over the age of eighteen and under the age of sixty were conscripted either for factories, essential jobs and nursing or for the Armed Forces. Those of us who volunteered for the Forces were either seventeen, or Irish, or colonials, or romantics like myself who could persuade an official to let them aboard a ship.[1]

One of the first things to be said about *All the Brave Promises* is that though it is weighty with an accumulation of authentic and eloquently evoked personal experience, an intense and powerful story, it is also one of her shortest full-length works, less than 200 pages; and, compared with her works of fiction, even the earliest ones, it is a firmly reticent work. Which is to say that the first-person narrator herself tells what she sees and feels, what happens and happens to her; bears witness, then, but without at any point, except most obliquely, establishing the kinds of outside connections and associations which are so characteristic of Settle's fiction. Some details above and beyond the limits of the book, some of the facts of her life before and after the war, are known. And these things enhance appreciation of the story. But mostly they are not in the book itself, which concentrates very tightly, in sharp focus, on the times and the events of the times, and on the remembered self who was witness to them, a character upon whom she fixes much more stringent limitations than she usually imposes on any fictional character. Partly this is no doubt a question of a natural modesty and, perhaps, a desire not to make any false claims for herself as having been at the (imaginary) bright center of things. A true war veteran, faithful to the hard facts, she makes no claims except the undeniable one that, like "Kilroy," she was there: "It is one small corner of this wartime life—

OTHER WORKS

the part of the Women's Auxiliary Air Force of the Royal Air Force in England—that I want to recall, perhaps to explain, to find out about, as I did then, step by step" (14). And this is precisely how she tells her tale, "step by step." Most of the story is told in a first-person, past-tense narration, strictly presentational, as the older and wiser woman who is telling the story presents what the young woman experienced and perceived without interference or commentary. Here she is, for example, walking across a little of London to the Kingsway recruiting station where she would be sworn in: "So, light as air, I swung past St. James Palace, sunken and small at the end of the street, and into the Mall, where across the wide, nearly deserted esplanade beyond its bordering trees St. James's Park lay veiled in the gray-green of October, air and trees almost translucent under the pale sun" (32).

But the truth is that all first-person stories are being told by someone who is at some distance or other, near or far, from both the events and the self who is presented and described. Characteristically, the first-person story has almost complete freedom in time and space. There is not really any narrative time but the present in a first-person story; for in such a story it is not the events themselves which constitute the action, but the telling of the tale. What is happening, and all that is happening, is that someone is telling a story. It therefore goes against the grain of the form to limit large parts of the narration to the purely "objective" perceptions of the speaker at a specific time and place and to concentrate on events, as if the speaker were, in fact, a third-person observer. The result of using the form in this way is to create an invisible tension in *All the Brave Promises*, a high degree of intensity at least somewhat separate from the inherent intensity of the events. Her story, as here remembered, is rich with anecdotes and events and characters, these latter much more on their own, as people are in wartime, without much past or future, without either the memories or hopes of the characters in her fictions. And most of them are without illusions. They are stripped down, essential characters who appear and disappear. The tension, the stress, what she calls the "overloading," gradually increases. It is for Settle, for the others, as it is for all combat survivors, a singular compound consciousness, an "edge, a full awakening, an adrenal heightening caused by fatigue and an atavistic sense of danger that made the senses expand and extend" (132). Thus, as is the case with the experience of modern warfare, only the leaders in command posts and distant places have any sense of "the big picture." For all the rest life (and death) is a series of small, chaotic moments, tight little scenes played out against a background of invisible and incredible stress. In *All the Brave Promises* there are moments of sudden, almost absurd contrast which make this same point dramatically. At one point, for example, she goes on a brief leave from her base and duties, invited, through personal connections, to enjoy a classic upper-class English country weekend. Here she comments on the conversation: "It was one of those easy, incestuous

OTHER WORKS

exchanges where Mountbatten is called Louis and a general with the deaths or lives of a million men at the tip of his pencil is called Bubby, or some such name" (114).

Settle communicates the feeling of the self, the individual, locked within the tightest limits by adhering closest of all to the sensuously realized and presented surfaces of things. Even so, it remains a story told some years later. And there are important moments when it is necessary for the mature wisdom and judgment of the speaker to be dissociated from the remembered self and the present moment to offer some comment on the action. From the outset Settle keeps this possibility alive by very lightly reminding the reader, from time to time, that the speaker is in fact remembering all this much later: "I can still recall, as hearing it again, the click of that washed, bare door closing" (33). The reader should note that to the speaker/teller of the tale, even the act of memory is primarily a sensuous affective experience, often only different from the original experience in its remove from it. Then, however, when it matters a great deal to articulate something which may have been deeply felt at the time, but was still essentially mysterious or even ineffable to her younger self, she is able to exercise her established right to enter into judgment; and she does so with much more impact than would be available if she had made a practice of regularly stepping into the story for exegetical purposes. Here, for instance, is one of those moments, a moment of complex truth not easily accessible to any of the participants at that time. Two sergeant pilots, home from Malta ("one of the worst services in the War"), have been assigned to the base in England where Settle is stationed. The following comment about the sergeants clearly comes from someone else, a mature speaker, who now knows much more than either the sergeants or the young women of the WAAF. Note that it is slightly elevated, raised by language and syntax to a more written, "literary," even judgmental style:

> They, their senses still charged to the outside capability of survival that humans can key to, had been set down, overstimulated and exhausted, in that idyllic little village to unwind slowly and realize that, for a little while, they had survived.
>
> That realization was not spoken but, from what they said, was like blood coming back into frozen fingers, gradually and with a painful joy; it was beginning to be experienced in the soft air of the afternoon—the resurging of halted life (90).

After a very brief prologue, "Recall," establishing the story as a work of memory, Settle goes swiftly into her story with only minimal background and expository information. It begins in Washington, DC, in 1942. Settle finds herself sharing a house with four English-women from the WAAF, code-and-cypher officers working in Washington. She decides to join the WAAF herself. In less than three full pages she is aboard the *City of Delhi* on the way from New York to Nova Scotia to join a convoy of a hundred ships guarded by two tiny

OTHER WORKS

Canadian corvettes, moving at a stately and dangerous four knots toward the war. Instantly there are characters of all kinds, and especially the young sailors she gets to know a little, here sketched quickly and memorably. And particularly a young Scotsman, Lofty, who joined up three years earlier at the age of fourteen and tries to tell her about war—"It's bloody dangerous" (25). London, a brief fling of final luxury, a stay at Claridge's. Meeting Lofty again together with two dozen Fleet Air Arm navigators, most too young to be served alcohol, in the bar at Claridge's. Ending abruptly with the narrator's interruption: "A year later I met one of them in a street in London. He said that all but four of the rest were dead" (30).

Sworn in, she boards a train headed north, sharing a compartment with East Enders, "six small Eliza Doolittles." Pausing at Reading, Settle reacts.

"Where's the jail?"
There was a dead silence. I watched the legs of the girl opposite, with the same gray surface of no sun and no scrubbing as all the others, feeling I had shouted.
She said, "There," proudly and pointed to, I think, a slightly higher red roof jutting above the rest.
"Know someone there?" That incredible cockney came across to me, interested.
"No. Only about someone."
"Me bruver's in there," she said and leaned back, comfortable against the seat.
The train pulled out of Reading station.
"Wot was he 'ad up for, the fellow you know about?" she

asked. I could almost see her toes wiggling with pleasure at someone to talk about to bridge the gap of strangeness. But I'm afraid Oscar Wilde had to let us down. "I don't know," I lied (35–36).

Already the basic counters of the literary game, pure elements of the experience as it will unfold, are in place. Not least of these is the humor which continues to appear in surprising places; distance—the Atlantic might as well be the Styx; danger—for the war is real and all around them, and people, large numbers of them, are dying in it. There is the clash of classes and cultures, to be modified but never really resolved. (In conversation Settle has described the English class system as "a lot like kudzu; no matter what you do, you can't get rid of it.") And she has already established her method of highly condensed, concentrated narrative presentation. She takes small views, focuses on small scenes and intense personal feelings. She goes into initial training at RAF Hereford. And the reader meets a crowd of characters. She is rapidly becoming a member of that crowd, even beginning to enjoy it, the victim of her own wishes and illusions: "I still had the illusion, common to artists at moments of registering concentration and to the isolated in cities, that I was observing all that was going on around me without being noticed, except by my own few comrades in despair, complaint and constant discomfort" (47). Not long after, she lost a certain amount of her self-confidence when she was badly treated by some of her peers, suddenly seized in

important turn, concentrating on a single extended episode. Settle, billeted for a time in a country house and often returning to quarters from her watch well after midnight, is suddenly overcome by panic, "blinded by terror." Searching for the cause of panic she finds what she identifies as "the center of greatest intensity." It is a tree, one of a pair of huge old trees. Friends, who feel nothing at all, take turns walking her past the pair of trees at night. Gradually the tree and its sense of terror "receded into dreams and nagging questions." In one of the very few violations of the tight time frame, Settle jumps ahead to show herself after the war returning to that same house and village to find the answer to her "nagging questions." There she is told by an aged local man, who knows the history of the place, that the frightening tree grows on the site of a gallows and the place where "the last hanging in chains in the west country" took place. At her peak of heightened awareness in the war, that high pitch of adrenalin and pure fatigue, she had not been wrong: "I had passed into the horror of the crowd, still soaking the ground around the tree" (145). Here, then, presented dramatically and without more comment, is Settle's physical discovery of one of the great truths which would come to shape her life's work in fiction: the real presence of the past, the power of the past to lay claim on the present. It is interesting that the year of the hanging, 1750, is close in time to the events of *O Beulah Land*; also that Settle's experience at the church at Burford, a similar awareness of the haunting life of the past, led to

OTHER WORKS

Prisons. It also serves to remind that this book, important as it may be in abstraction as one among the finest books dealing with World War II (the latest British paperback edition quotes the distinguished critic Alan Pryce-Jones, naming it as "one of the few really good books to come out of the Second World War"), is also a subtle portrait of the artist as a young woman, learning what matters, being broken by war finally, but clearly at the same time coming together as a whole being.

The final brief chapters chronicle the outward and visible disintegration of her unit and her fellows and herself. Morale sags; clashes occur; and there is a hardening of the "cold and brutal division between officers and other ranks" (170). There is a series of acts of injustice, growing in seriousness. Moments of brief and hopeless little "rebellions" against all that, and then, quickly, in a matter of weeks, the symptoms of her "signals shock," the results of months of listening for voices through the ceaseless enemy jamming, are clear and evident. It was, she writes, "a classic disintegration":

Into the enemy jamming which, by now, was never out of my waking mind, fake messages began to intrude, as they had to my watch mate when she was asleep. The messages drifted over from dreams to the edge of my hearing, to the watch itself, and in the night, lulled by the hours before morning, in the trancelike waiting, I would suddenly hear calls for help out of the night ether, "Hello, Darky. Hello, Darky," and I would clutch the set to tune in aural visions—

nothing there but the night and my own anxiety for action (174).

Then, suddenly, it is all over. She's off to London on sick leave and on the way out of the service:

In civilian clothes that no longer fitted, with a one-way pass to London, three pounds ten and my "ticket"—my discharge—in my pocket, I was on the way to the American Office of War Information in London, the cocktail parties, the conferences, the PX cigarettes, the frenetic turmoil of people who had names and thought they were running the juggernaut of war, which was only spending itself toward its own death like a great tiring unled beast" (176).

Since *All the Brave Promises*, and except for interviews and her extended piece for *Contemporary Authors Autobiography Series*, Settle has so far written very few personal-memory pieces. A significant and relevant exception is "How Pleasant to Meet Mr. Eliot," written for the *New York Times Book Review* in 1984, partly in response to a recent unauthorized biography of Eliot and the Broadway play *Tom and Viv*. It is not precisely a correction: "None of us can set the record straight. We see from where we stand and remember what we knew."[2] Brief as it is, this piece tells us a good deal about Eliot's kindness to and compassion for others, and it presents an unflinching self-portrait of the artist in 1946 beginning her "eight years of catch-as-catch-can or freelance journalism before I sold a novel." Describing the mood of the time, she typically begins with

OTHER WORKS

sensuous, particular impressions, moving slowly toward generalizations. Those general truths say it all in a few clauses: "When the war had gone on too long, and the right and wrong of its beginning had drifted into the pragmatic, terrible decisions at its end; when the voices we had trusted sounded shrill and we knew we had been fooled but didn't know quite how and were too old for our years, . . . we longed for assurance," she writes. She had found it in the *Four Quartets*, especially in "Little Gidding," which she shrewdly sees as a major poem of the war. "The accepted premise is that little poetry truly reflects World War II. But there is 'Little Gidding.' " And, of course, Settle has a physical image for the impact of Eliot's poetry on her generation. "He had led us through a mine field, stripped of whatever communal illusions were left over from a more innocent time. Then he had the miraculous effrontery of spirit to promise that 'all shall be well.' "

Taken together with *All the Brave Promises*, the memory of meeting Eliot, tells us a great deal about the spirit of Settle at the beginning of her search for her voice and subject. Most importantly it confirms that, wounded and toughened and disillusioned as she may have been, she had already passed beyond fashionable cynicism, a response to reality which she would ever after seek to stifle if not reject.

Miscellaneous Journalism

Following her late popular recognition and the subsequent honors of various kinds which came to her for and after *Blood Tie*, Settle has now returned from time to time to journalism, as a writer with now a more or less public name and a body of serious work which could be, perhaps, enhanced or diminished by her nonfiction work. That is, after *Blood Tie* won the National Book Award she was in a position where her name, in and of itself, would be of some interest to both editors and readers. That she has neither abused this new interest with frivolous, ephemeral pieces nor allowed herself to be inhibited from writing about what interests her has resulted in a number of genuinely worthwhile journalistic pieces, pieces which are closely related to her own work and concerns in a number of ways and are thus pertinent to this brief study.

In addition to the personal and autobiographical pieces already cited, her recent journalistic work is of several kinds. There are travel articles, written out of the background of the Beulah quintet and her American novels,[3] and there are others which appear to have been part of the research and preparation for *Celebration*. There are pieces directly dealing with particular personalities in show business and the popular arts, written for the "Arts and Leisure" section of the Sunday *New York Times*.[4] There are a few, a very few, book reviews.[5] Finally there are a few particular pieces evidently done

OTHER WORKS

out of a sense of duty or of political and social commitment.

Of this last kind there is her already mentioned address to the American Writers Congress in October, 1981, where she discussed the forms of literary censorship against which the contemporary American writer must contend. Shortly after the elections of 1984 she joined with a group of poets and writers at Northwestern University, under the sponsorship of *TriQuarterly* magazine, in a politically oriented symposium loosely titled "The Writer in Our World." With the others she gave a reading from her work, participated in panel discussions (and arguments), and delivered a formal presentation, an expansion and development of her earlier American Writers Congress talk: "Facets of Censorship."[6] Here she spoke out strongly against three kinds of literary censorship which, she argued, serve to inhibit contemporary writers: personal censorship ("a thing to be watched in the room like the devil"); commercial censorship, which she defined as the way the business practices of American publishing tend to let the books which have less commercial prospects sink or swim, without much aid or comfort from the publisher, most of whose resources are devoted to the exploitation of "blockbusters" and the preservation of the more successful titles on the backlist. And finally she attacked what she called aesthetic censorship, which she defined as a kind of disguised elitism, combining the disdain of the intellectuals for much of popular culture, especially popular literature, and, more significantly, the contemptuous refusal of too many American intellectuals to take ordinary people seriously. "We simply must go out to meet those who are less articulate than ourselves" (249).

There were things which she refused to tolerate or endorse. One of these was the distortion or the blithe ignorance of hard facts. In conversation she has strongly endorsed Robert Frost's celebrated line from "Mowing"—"The fact is the sweetest dream that labor knows." She obviously does not feel that her principles are in any way compromised by factual accuracy. The artist who sentenced herself to the hard labor of research for the Beulah quintet would not take factual foolishness lightly. At one point, for example, in the midst of a heated discussion of the Vietnam war, most of it carried on by people who were veterans of no wars, she felt compelled to remind them of the deep difference between the soldier and all kinds of outside observers: "There is an almost unbridgeable gulf between the person who has joined the forces and cannot get out, who is expected to obey orders, who is expected to stay within a system which is a wartime system, and anyone, anyone, watching it for any reason. This is a gulf so profound that it's almost, as I say, impossible to talk about" (226). In another discussion she may have offended rigid feminists by her use of the touchstone of personal experience, the experience of being in the WAAF. "In the whole experience that I had," she says, "I never saw the feeling of power or the feeling toward war as a prerogative of either sex. It was individual with

OTHER WORKS

people. You've never seen a sergeant until you've seen a female sergeant full of a sense of domination over people" (254–55). Settle surprised some of the others with a compassionate plea: "I've been listening to the moral dilemma of the United States right now, and a great deal of it in terms of its extremes—someplace else, some other time, some other death. I would ask us not necessarily to be kinder to ourselves right now, but to understand in terms of our history—and some histories are like other histories—that we're tired right now" (281). It would have been ever so much easier, more comfortable, to mouth platitudes and clichés. Or at least nod wise approval. But Settle is far too independent for anything like that. She will always speak up. As she said in her address to the American Writers Congress: "If the strength of liberal thinking is the open mind, its weakness, too often and too early, is the closed mouth."[7]

A stronger political symposium was the volume put together by editor and writer Earl Shorris in association with *The Nation* magazine—*While Someone Else Is Eating*. Here ten writers undertook to deal with the subject of American poverty in the time of the Reagan administration. The contribution of Settle, "Coalburg, Virginia: One of the Lucky Ones," is at once radical and daring.[8] It tells the story (as a work of fiction) of the narrator's cousin Edgar, a dedicated conservative in life and lifestyle and a dedicated employee, in management, of a subsidiary of the Company, a chemical company located "in one of those company towns that stretch along the narrow mountain valleys of West Virginia." With many sharp and satirical observations she follows his rise and fall when, to his shock and dismay, in 1981 the subsidiary closes down, and he and everybody else are out of their jobs. It is a sad and witty little story. In an afterword to the piece Settle makes it clear why she has chosen this particular story for this particular anthology. "It is easy to convince the convinced," she writes, "and to sympathize with the sympathetic. What I have tried to do in this story is to draw attention to another kind of economic neglect. . . . It is fiction because I wanted to reflect in it, from fragments of observation, the lives of a whole body of 'good Americans' at management level who are doubly forgotten."

Her independence of mind and her willingness to try to say outright what she means are manifest in her literary criticism. Most of her theoretical literary ideas are to be derived directly from her work or from the various interviews and personal pieces wherein she declares her allegiances, loyalty to her masters—especially and consistently to Conrad, Stendahl, Tolstoi, Turgenev, Proust. But there are occasional book reviews where she also speaks her piece. Reviewing Norman Mailer's *Ancient Evenings*, Settle surprised some people by praising the book highly.[9] It has been harshly criticized by some reviewers, and she acknowledged some validity in their reservations: "Yes, there is copraphilia, necrophilia, incest, sodomy, bestiality, and more varieties of sado-masochistic sex than are found in de Sade. This is a weakness in the book because it is the only part which clings to modern morality. Mailer has always

UNDERSTANDING MARY LEE SETTLE

A later essay written for the *New York Times Book Review*, "Recapturing the Past in Fiction," while an invaluable guide to the process of making the Beulah quintent, also deals more generally with both the problems and the possible triumphs of the historical novel.[11] There are the matters of general aphoristic rules and guidelines. "By its nature, history is bound in time; fiction is timeless when it reaches the reality of a person, an act or a scene that transcends the words conveying it." "Both time and space are distances, and they work for historians and novelists in the same way—not as a gulf, but as a psychic focus. Hindsight—which revises, tears down, discovers trends and explains by concept— has little place in fiction." "Historians find facts and shape theories; novelists find facts and make fiction." "Both history and the novel rely on the principle of selection. Where they part is that the writer of fiction must become so contemporary that the view is not simply of what happened, but of what people thought was happening at the time." "The present in which the writer writes, no matter how far in the past the subject may be, is reflected in the selection of the subject. The years when I was writing informed the past I chose." And there are the matters of personal experience as, book by book, she tells how the vision of the Beulah quintet arrived and how the books finally came to be.

Closely associated with all of her novels sharing an American setting is a series of pieces Settle wrote on assignment for the travel section of the *New York Times*. All these pieces are elegantly executed, but none of seemingly "objective" presentation the key elements of exposition. Handled this way, information itself becomes a matter of some suspense and in its own way is as "objective" as the fallen leaves, the cold, the two old men trying to run to each other's arms. Who are they? Why are they running and embracing in tears? Then when she has answered those questions and pulled back, almost cinematically, to the silent observing escort on horseback, the peak of the drama and the point where many another writer would have closed the scene, she suddenly introduces the final touch—the sound of sobbing, sourceless. Who is it—someone among the escort? The narrator? The reader? All of the above?

There are also the speeches, interviews, and essays which came after her recognition and honors and which might be described as professional pieces, part of her effort as a public figure, in the literary world at least, to pay her dues, to perform some service for the benefit of other artists who are just at the beginning of their careers or, perhaps, mature writers not so fortunate as herself. Most of these things are almost wholly ephemeral, even where texts of tape recordings or videotapes exist. But there is one essay, "Works of Art or Power Tools?" which summarizes much of her concern for the contemporary literary situation, including aspects of the publishing industry and of the ways and means of the public recognition of artists.[13] Its title refers to the January 1979 U.S. Supreme Court decision in Thor Power Tool Company v. Commissioner of Internal Revenue, which allowed for the taxation of inventories. One result of this decision was to discourage commercial publishers from maintaining a large backlist of books in print and, indeed, from warehousing for long any books other than outstanding best sellers. Together with contemporary marketing practices and the new ways that publishing houses are managed, this has added up to a serious danger to the literature, if any, of the future. Lost in this system, as she viewed it, would be all the fine writers like herself who took a long time finding their audience. She gains more impact by using examples not of herself and her contemporaries but from literary history: "Would this, by the standards of modern commercial publishing and the IRS, have been reason to suppress, or to shred after one year, the works of George Eliot, Thackeray, Emily and Charlotte Brontë?" There is in this essay one discreet, slightly oblique, personal point which, considering her own history, is of more than passing interest. "The novelist requires, in order to work," she writes, "an atmosphere of possibility. Novels have been written in spite of noise, poverty, and constant demands on time, which are the prime enemies of writers. But to write without a hope of reaching a reader is destructive to conception itself. Mark Rothko said that a painting died from not being looked at. A novel can die of hopelessness in the brain of its creator."

Coming from a writer who was somehow brave enough and strong enough (and lucky enough) to keep hope alive in the face of times of severe discouragement, this is, for other writers, a charitable and understanding observation and not one that is usually made by those whose fortune has finally improved. For the reader it can serve as a warning. Much that might have been valuable has been lost or wasted in our time.

Settle has published very few short stories. There is the short fiction "Coalburg, Virginia: One of the Lucky Ones," created for *While Someone Else Is Eating*, and "Paragraph Eleven," which was in fact an excerpt from *All the Brave Promises*. In 1954 she published "Congress Burney," in *The Paris Review*.[14] It is directly related to the American themes and stories which would obsess her for so many years. A grown woman returns to the scene of her childhood and summons up the memory of a poor tenant family in the Depression and their story from the few fragments they have left behind them (as in *The Killing Ground*), learning from her aunt one crucial piece of information she had never suspected. There are many touches which would come to be characteristic of her later work and any number of links to the Beulah quintet. And there is a moment in which the narrator, a Settle surrogate, has tripped over an abandoned wagon wheel and thinks for a moment of the family, the Burneys, who had been there:

They'd always trick you like that, trick you into remembering them when you were about to give even their fragments up for lost. That's what they were made of; of fragments lost in the general tiredness, like promises of diamonds in the dung, and those bright tricks would catch you in your mind's eye in places halfway across the world when the sun would fling a long shadow across London or a Paris street the Burneys never heard of, and Congress would rise up from the shadow, moseying along the back road to Cow Horn at supper-time, kicking the dust" (117).

Somehow it is all there, the Beulah quintet and *Celebration*, the sense of subject and themes as well as suggestions of method; and the language, a blending of styles, the written and spoken. Tightly condensed though it is, the story seems leisurely. Simple and straightforward on the level of action, it is dense, weighty with a past and with living memories. And there are, as there will be throughout her fiction, the sudden allusions, apt for the first-person narrator but nonetheless surprising, which like a startling simile or metaphor lift the mundane toward the mythical. Here, following a detailed, photographic description of Congress Burney, "a long lank spare-boned hillbilly," she moves in the present, recalling him to something more: "But now as I see him, he had a kind of pride about him—that and silence that made you remember him. He had deep, dark eyes set back in their sockets so that they had the look of Rembrandt's old rabbi, a little flicker of fierceness left, but sad beyond hope" (121).

"The Old Wives' Tale," published in *Harper's Magazine* and later selected for the annual O. Henry collection, has the same kind of density and allusive force—in this case the myth of Persephone which is directly recalled and revised by a speaker.[15] Here is the first-person story of a young woman, returning by ship from Europe to America (and Virginia, West Virginia), who meets an old lady on board, someone from the same part of America who tells her a three-part story of lost love, the lovers' last chance to be together alone ruined by a sudden storm that makes a river between them impassable. Here again is the kind of allusion which, by likeness and contrast, gives the tale a deep resonance:

"Then through all that rain and wind I saw him on the other side and he saw me. Neither of us even waved. What was the use? He just stood there like some mute Dante who would never write a line, just ship coal and dream; and me a middle-aged plump little Beatrice, soaked and bedraggled, with her hair half down, who knew when she was whipped" (78).

Except for the fact that she has been so busy writing her novels, it is something of a mystery why Settle has not published more stories. These stories have great strength and originality. It may be that latter quality which has discouraged her from continuing with short fiction. For her stories, though highly controlled and well made, are also highly unfashionable. Throughout her career the fashionable direction of the American story has been toward increasing abstraction and minimalism. Her people do not live or act in isolation. They have pasts like shadows and they have futures. There is always a sense of life going on outside the limits of the story. There have been very few editors in the world of commercial or literary magazines whose training or habits have prepared them for that kind of story. Perhaps now that she has name and reputation enough to overcome easy objections, she will return to the form.

Finally there are three other books of nonfiction, neither unimportant nor irrelevant, but, as Settle has said, written mainly for the money to enable her to gain the time to write her novels. They were also intended, at least originally, for a juvenile audience. The first of these, *The Story of Flight* (1967), is a book she is not happy with. She explains that it had to be written in a language (for seven-year-olds) which proved too confining for her. She speaks of it as unsuccessful in all details except for her account of the flight of Charles Lindbergh, where, she says, the limitations of the language worked to her advantage.

The Scopes Trial: The State of Tennessee v. John Thomas Scopes (1972), written for the "young adult" category of juvenile books, is a superb accounting of the background and the events of the theatrical trial staged in Dayton, Tennessee, in the summer of 1925. The narrative arrangement is balanced, intense, and basically dramatic. Some of the intensity, or engagement by Settle, may come from the fact that there is a personal connection. She is kin to John Scopes. But it has a built-in intensity as well, for the trial was a drama of the highest order. A drama of personalities, the two old men, public figures: William Jennings Bryan, thirty years at the center of national American politics, three times a strong candidate for president, the Great Commoner; and his antagonist, Clarence Darrow, one of the best-known lawyers of his time and in American history, a flamboyant figure of passionate and skeptical intelligence. Although her intellectual sympathies are with the defense, with the American Civil Liberties Union and not with the Fundamentalists, she has the novelist's emotional empathy to understand and feel for Bryan as his clash with Darrow turned into a disastrous defeat:

> Stripped away from Bryan were all his protections of fame and brilliance, his fantastic talent as an orator, and the love of his followers. He sat before intelligence, the one attribute he had ignored, belittled, and hidden from since he, the unquestioning son of a small-town Puritan father, had succeeded as Americans succeed, through being popular— like the heroes of Horatio Alger and a thousand matinees— as a defender of the right, his country, and his God.
> It was a slaughter.[16]

She re-creates the weather and the feel of things and, above all, the sense of where these small, highly local though widely publicized events fit into the context of our history, earlier and later. And at the conclusion she allows herself a summary of the implications of the story. Seeing "the freezing fear of change" as the link between the long-gone Fundamentalists and later, "more sinister" troubles, the McCarthy era and after, she relates its meaning to society in general:

For democracy, unlike any other modern form of government, uses the ability to change, to bend without breaking,

OTHER WORKS

as one of its great strong sources of energy. It is the one form of government that thrives on questions. There will always be those who fear this quality, who will yearn to flee to the safety of dogma, for the war between the security of blind acceptance and the insecurity of intelligent questioning is international and is never-ending (113).

There is another significant connection to her major work. In her chapter on the American Civil Liberties Union she uses the occasion to quote from the seventeenth-century Puritan martyr John Lilburne, whose words before the Star Chamber in 1638 ("For what is done to any one may be done to every one") have become the motto of the ACLU, and served as a personal inspiration to Thomas Jefferson and, finally, for herself in the creation of *Prisons*. She recounts Lilburne's story briefly in her "Foreword" to the novel.

Most recently there is *Water World* (1984). This is a fascinating little book, in part the result of research for both *Blood Tie* and *Celebration*, in part the fruit of her own personal experience of scuba diving. As she writes on the book jacket: "I learned to scuba dive in the Aegean Sea, off Turkey. I had been afraid of the water, but when I dived into the beautiful undersea world, my fears were forgotten. It is because of that discovery and the wonders of it that I have written this book." Written with casual, stylish precision, handsomely illustrated, it is an extended essay on the subject of the sea, its history, its science, its legends and creatures, gracefully informed by her diving experiences. It opens and closes with an appeal to the reader to join in an *imaginative* enterprise,

to engage senses, feeling, and thought to move toward
the pleasure of understanding what can be understood.
It opens also, in the first chapter, "Blue Globe," with the
picture of the world as seen by an astronaut (as it is seen
at the high point of *Celebration*). Her expressed view of
the sea is much the same as her view of the earth as a
whole, full of ancient mystery, layers of the coming and
going of creatures, including man, and not so much a
plea as strong counsel to cherish and preserve it. Her
advice to the beginning diver might be taken, as well, as
an invitation to the reader who wishes to explore her
art, her life's work:

You are ready to go into the sea world and stay for a
while. If you have learned to dive carefully, you will have a
wonderful sense of weightlessness and peace. You are not
going there to grab, or disturb, or destroy. You are going to
see a tiny part of the underwater world. It has no national
boundaries; it has only the natural changes of undersea
scape. It is both hospitable and indifferent, and nothing
there cares what you are trying to prove. Just go. Go gently,
go slowly, go politely. Go there to wander and begin to understand.[17]

Notes

1. Settle, *All the Brave Promises* (New York: Seymour
Lawrence/Delacorte, 1966), 15.

2. Settle, "How Pleasant to Meet Mr. Eliot," *New York Times Book
Review* 16 Dec. 1984: 11.

OTHER WORKS

3. "The Paths to America's Promised Land: A Novelist Returns to Her Beulah Land," *New York Times* 1 Aug. 1982, sec. 10: 15, 22; "Mr. Jefferson's World," *New York Times Magazine: The Sophisticated Traveler* 13 Mar., 1983: 123–24, 126, 128; "Carried Back to Old Virginia: The Great Houses along the James River Bear Witness to 400 Years of Social History," *New York Times* 27 May 1984, sec. 10: 14, 17; "Hidden Places in the Virginias' Spa Country: Finding Comforts of an Older South," *New York Times* 15 June 1986, sec. 10: 19, 40; "Mary Lee Settle," in "Writers Savor Christmas Memories," *New York Times* 24 Dec. 1986, C1, 3.

4. See, e.g., "Bobby Short: Keys to a Lyrical Life," *New York Times* 7 Dec. 1986, sec. 2: 1, 20.

5. In addition to those discussed here see: "This Land Was His Land," rev. of *Woody Guthrie: A Life*, by Joe Klein, *New York Times Book Review* 7 Dec. 1980: 3, 26–27; "White to Black to Redneck: Missionary among All Minorities," rev. of *Will Campbell and the Soul of the South*, by Thomas L. Connelly, *Los Angeles Times* "Book Review," 29 Aug. 1982: 1; "The Dignity and Ties of Apron-String America," rev. of *Growing Up*, by Russell Baker, *Los Angeles Times* "Book Review 10 Oct. 1982": 1, 10.

6. *The Writer in Our World: A Symposium Sponsored by "TriQuarterly" Magazine*, ed. Reginald Gibbons (Boston: Atlantic Monthly Press, 1986), 245–49.

7. Tape Cassette, Culture Industry, American Writers Congress, 9–12 Oct., 1981, New York City.

8. *While Someone Else Is Eating*, ed. Earl Shorris (Garden City: Anchor-Doubleday, 1984) 52–58.

9. Settle, rev. of *Ancient Evenings*, by Norman Mailer, *Los Angeles Times* "Book Review" 24 Apr. 1983: 1.

10. Settle, "Novels of History and Imagination," *New York Times Book Review* 3 Oct. 1982: 9, 18.

11. Settle, "Recapturing the Past in Fiction," *New York Times Book Review* 12 Feb. 1984: 1, 36–37.

12. Settle, "Mr. Jefferson's World" 124, 126.

13. Settle, "Works of Art or Power Tools?" *Virginia Quarterly*

Review (1981): 1–14. See also Settle, "Book Awards," *America* 1–8 Sept. 1984: 110–14.

14. Settle, "Congress Burney." *Paris Review* 7 (1954–55): 114–29.

15. Settle, "The Old Wives' Tale," *Harper's Magazine* Sept. 1955: 73–78.

16. Settle, *The Scopes Trial* (New York: Watts, 1972), 106.

17. Settle, *Water World* (New York: Dutton, 1984), 41.

CONCLUSION

What next? In a final interview she tells the author: "Now with *Celebration* finished, I am now ready to write another book. And this concept began with thinking about Stendahl and thinking about the change of the concept of love, as obsessive, romantic love, not Christian love. And I knew somehow that what Stendahl said about love did not apply to actual experience. We don't live in the same drawing rooms. We don't have the same great gulf between men and women. And then I began to think of a past experience in which there was a triangle, but instead of it being two men and a woman or two women and a man, it was a far deeper, archetypal triangle than that. The triangle was mother-son-lover (woman). And this concept—and I've got it down here as a date, on July 25th, 1986, with an exclamation point after it—became an image."

Then she reads the image at the heart of the new novel from her working notebook:

"This is the way it begins—an image. It has always

been this way. Until there is an image there is no story.

"A woman sits in the front seat of a car. Smell of leather and tobacco smoke and rain. The motor idles. The windshield wipers move back and forth, back and forth, *click* and *click* and *click*, a metronome that gives the image an interior rhythm, a timing. But there is no time. That could be illusion. Where she is, where the car is, the street, the town, the night, there is no time. It is there, the image to call forth from a timeless center, relived always, at first faintly as a dream, then within its temperament, its senses. Smell of tobacco, rain, linen and night. The woman sits there, neither within nor without time, but remembered, recalled. She answers without speaking. She is there, her hands in her lap, watching the rain, herded by the wipers that break and scatter the streetlights and the pavement sleek with night rain. She is not smiling, but she exists within a patience that is happy, weightless, light, floating, willing to want, to trust. What? What and why? The demands. The question. She has become, by this, a woman in illusive time, a story, a love story. Not to explain, but to explore love. And so . . . an adventure."

BIBLIOGRAPHY

Works by Mary Lee Settle

Books

The Love Eaters. New York: Harper, 1954; London: Heinemann, 1954.

The Kiss of Kin. New York: Harper, 1955; London: Heinemann, 1955.

O Beulah Land. New York: Viking, 1956; London: Heinemann, 1956.

Know Nothing. New York: Viking, 1960; London: Heinemann, 1961.

Fight Night on a Sweet Saturday. New York: Viking, 1964; London: Heinemann, 1965.

All the Brave Promises: Memoirs of Aircraft Woman 2nd Class 2146391. New York: Seymour Lawrence/Delacorte, 1966; London: Heinemann, 1966.

The Story of Flight. New York: Random House, 1967. Juvenile.

The Clam Shell. New York: Seymour Lawrence/Delacorte, 1971; London: Bodley Head, 1972.

The Scopes Trial: The State of Tennessee v. John Thomas Scopes. New York: Watts, 1972. Juvenile.

Prisons. New York: Putnam, 1973; published as *The Long Road to Paradise*, London: Constable, 1974.

Blood Tie. Boston: Houghton Mifflin, 1977.

The Scapegoat. New York: Random House, 1980.

The Killing Ground. New York: Farrar, Straus, 1982.

Water World. New York: Dutton, 1984. Juvenile.

Celebration. New York: Farrar, Straus, 1986.

UNDERSTANDING MARY LEE SETTLE

Short Fiction and Excerpts

"Congress Burney." *Paris Review* 7 (1954–1955): 114–29.

"The Old Wives' Tale." *Harper's Magazine* Sept. 1955: 73–78; reprinted in *Prize Stories 1957: The O. Henry Awards*. Ed. Paul Engle (Garden City: Doubleday, 1957): 241–61.

"Paragraph Eleven." *The Girl in the Black Raincoat*. Ed. George Garrett (New York: Duell, Sloan, 1966): 103–08.

"Excerpt from Novel-in-Progress." *Blue Ridge Review 1* (1978): 26–31.

"Coalburg, Virginia: One of the Lucky Ones." *While Someone Else Is Eating*. Ed. Earl Shorris (Garden City: Anchor-Doubleday, 1984): 52–58.

Personal and Autobiographical

"The Editor's Room." *Sweet Briar College Alumnae Magazine* Fall 1978: 34–35.

"Mary Lee Settle." *Contemporary Authors Autobiography Series*. Vol. 1. Ed. Dedria Bryfonski. Detroit: Gale Research, 1984. 307–23.

"Recapturing the Past in Fiction." *New York Times Book Review* 12 Feb. 1984: 1, 36–37.

"How Pleasant to Meet Mr. Eliot." *New York Times Book Review* 16 Dec. 1984: 10–11.

"Mary Lee Settle." "Writers Savor Christmas Memories." *New York Times* 24 Dec. 1986: C1, 3.

"A Special Message for the First Edition from Mary Lee Settle." *Celebration*. The Signed First Edition Society; Franklin Center, PA: Franklin Library, 1986.

"Life Is Really a Dance." *U.S. News and World Report* 22 Dec. 1986: 64.

BIBLIOGRAPHY

Critical Pieces and Book Reviews

"Acceptance Speech: National Book Award/Fiction/1978." Palaemon Broadside 9. Winston-Salem, NC: Palaemon Press, 1978.

"A Salute to the Thirtieth National Book Awards." *Publishers' Publicity Association*, 1979.

"This Land Was His Land." Rev. of *Woody Guthrie: A Life*, by Joe Klein. *New York Times Book Review* 7 Dec. 1980: 3, 26–27.

"Works of Art or Power Tools?" *Virginia Quarterly Review 57 (1981): 1–14.*

"White to Black to Redneck: Missionary among All Minorities." Rev. of *Will Campbell and the Soul of the South*, by Thomas L. Connelly. *Los Angeles Times*, "Book Review" 29 Aug. 1982: 1.

"Novels of History and Imagination." Rev. of *The Sea Runners*, by Ivan Doig, and *The Barefoot Brigade*, by Douglas C. Jones. *New York Times Book Review* 3 Oct. 1982: 9, 18.

"The Dignity and Ties of Apron-String America." Rev. of *Growing Up*, by Russell Baker. *Los Angeles Times*, "Book Review" 10 Oct. 1982: 1, 10.

"Ancient Evenings." Rev. of *Ancient Evenings*, by Norman Mailer. *Los Angeles Times*, "Book Review" 24 Apr. 1983: 1.

"Book Awards." *America*. 1–8 Sept. 1984: 110–14.

"Writers in Academia: Disciplined Schizophrenia." *AWP Newsletter* Sept. 1984: 9.

"Facets of Censorship." *The Writer in Our World: A Symposium Sponsored by "TriQuarterly" Magazine*. Ed. Reginald Gibbons. Boston: Atlantic Monthly Press, 1986. 245–49.

Travel and Other Essays

"The Paths to America's Promised Land: A novelist Returns to Her Beulah Land." *New York Times*, 1 Aug. 1982, sec. 10: 15, 22.

"Mr. Jefferson's World." *New York Times Magazine: The Sophisticated Traveler* 13 Mar. 1983: 123–24, 126, 128.

"Carried Back to Old Virginia: The Great Houses along the James River Bear Witness to 400 Years of Social History." *New York Times*, 27 May 1984, sec. 10: 14, 17.

"Atlas of a Writer's World." *New York Times Magazine: The Sophisticated Traveler* 6 Oct. 1985: 28–29.

"First Glimpses of the Ancient Imperial City: Finding the Calm among the Crowds." *New York Times* 27 Apr. 1986, sec. 10: 15, 32.

"Hidden Places in the Virginias' Spa Country: Finding comforts of an Older South," *New York Times*. 15 June 1986, Sec. 10: 19, 40.

"Glass and Steel Gild the Heart of Hong Kong." *New York Times* 14 Sept. 1986, Sec. 10: 15, 26.

"Bobby Short: Keys to a Lyrical Life." *New York Times* 7 Dec. 1986, sec. 2: 1, 20.

Critical Works about Mary Lee Settle

There is as yet no bibliography of Mary Lee Settle's work. And at this writing there is no book-length study of her work.

Articles and Essays

Bain, Robert. "Mary Lee Settle." *Southern Writers: A Biographical Dictionary*. Ed. Robert Bain, Joseph M. Flora,

BIBLIOGRAPHY

and Louis D. Rubin, Jr. Baton Rouge: Louisiana State University Press, 1979. 404. Brief biographical entry containing some information, particularly concerning her parents (Rachel Tompkins Settle and Joseph Edward Settle) not found elsewhere.

Betts, Doris. Review of *Celebration*. *America*, 18 Oct. 1986: 211–12. This short essay review by an outstanding contemporary novelist is probably the most thoughtful treatment of *Celebration*.

Canfield, Rosemary M. "The Beulah Quintet." *Masterplots II: American Fiction Series*. Ed. Frank N. McGill. Englewood Cliffs, NJ: Salem Press, 1986. 151–60. In spite of its context in this uneven reference series, this is a serious and able discussion of the quintet, the most thorough so far. Especially good at pointing out some of the complex and subtle unifying elements in the five novels.

Contemporary Literary Criticism. Ed. Sharon R. Gunton. Detroit: Gale Research, 1981. Vol 19: 408–12. A selection of excerpts from critical response to Settle's work through *The Scapegoat*.

Garrett, George. "Mary Lee Settle's Beulah Land Trilogy." *Rediscoveries*. Ed. David Madden. New York: Crown, 1971. 171–78. This piece, written before the trilogy had turned into the quintet, is of interest mainly as dealing with the place of Settle and her art in the 1970s.

———. "An Invitation to the Dance: A Few Words on the Art of Mary Lee Settle." *Blue Ridge Review* 1 (1978): 18–24. A personal tribute to and appreciation of the work of Settle.

———. "Mary Lee Settle." *Dictionary of Literary Biography: American Novelists since World War II* 2nd series. Ed. James E. Kibler, Jr. Detroit: Gale Research/Bruccoli Clark, 1980. 281–89. Written and published before Settle had completed the Beulah quintet, this essay is now somewhat out of date, but still contains a number of useful quotations from the personal correspondence of Settle with Garrett.

Houston, Robert. "Blood Sacrifice." *The Nation.* 8 Nov. 1980: 469–71. A sensitive and intelligent essay review of *The Scapegoat* by a novelist who has himself written of the history of the American labor movement. "When you finish *The Scapegoat*," he writes, "you know how it felt to be alive in 1912 during a coal miner's strike in West Virginia."

Joyner, Nancy Carol. "Mary Lee Settle's Connections: Class and Clothes in the Beulah Quintet." *Women Writers of the Contemporary South.* Ed. Peggy Whitman Prenshaw. Jackson: University Press of Mississippi, 1984. 165–78. Close reading of the quintet to show how deftly and subtly Settle handles the clash of social classes and how carefully she costumes her characters so that clothing assumes symbolic values.

O'Hara, J. D. "What Rogue Elephants Know." *The Nation* 20 May 1978: 605–06. In the form of an essay review of *Blood Tie*, this piece is also a spirited defense of Settle's art against those critics who felt that her National Book Award was undeserved.

Schafer, William J. "Mary Lee Settle's Beulah Quintet: History Darkly, Through a Single-Lens Reflex." *Appalachian Journal* 10 (1982): 77–86. A mixed critical reaction to the Beulah quintet. He questions the depth and accuracy of some of her research.

Tape Cassettes

Mary Lee Settle Reads the Beulah Quintet (excerpts). American Audio Prose Library 2131, 1982.

BIBLIOGRAPHY

Mary Lee Settle: Interview. American Audio Prose Library 2132, 1982.

Culture Industry. American Writers Congress, 9–12 Oct. 1981, New York City.

Selected Interviews

Amorese, Cynthia H. "Mary Lee Settle." *Commonwealth: The Magazine of Virginia* Jan. 1981: 45–51.

Coburn, Randy Sue. "Life Sings So Sweetly For Settle." *The Washington Star*, 16 Nov. 1980, F1, 6.

Heumann, Joe. "An Interview with Mary Lee Settle." *The Daily Iowan* (Iowa City) 16 Apr. 1976: 10B.

Johnson, Janice. "Settle's Fiction: Asking Why." *The Cavalier Daily* (University of Virginia) 18 Nov. 1980: 1.

Kerr, Tim. "Author: Novelist Settle Maintains Success without Catering to 'Fashions.' " *The Daily Progress* (Charlottesville, VA.) 30 Oct. 1986: D6.

MacPherson, Myra. "Mary Lee Settle, Forthrightly." *The Washington Post* 15 Jan. 1987: C9.

Morgan, John G. "West Virginian of the Year for 1978." *Sunday Gazette-Mail* (Charleston), 7 Jan. 1979: M2–4.

Neal, G. Dale. "Filling an Empty Room—The Art of Mary Lee Settle." *Student* (Wake Forest University) Spring 1980: 18–22.

Ryan, William F. "Mary Lee Settle and Johnny Rebel." *Virginia Country* May/June 1984: 53–59.

Shattuck, Roger. "A Talk with Mary Lee Settle." *New York Times Book Review* 26 Oct. 1980: 43–46.

Taormina, C. A. "On Time with Mary Lee Settle." *Blue Ridge Review* 1 (1978): 8–17.

INDEX

INDEX

INDEX

INDEX

INDEX

INDEX

INDEX

INDEX

INDEX

INDEX

INDEX

INDEX

Works

INDEX

INDEX

INDEX